T0056903

POCKET GUIDE TO

PREPPING

SUPPLIES

MORE THAN 200 ITEMS
YOU CAN'T BE WITHOUT

PATTY HAHNE

Skyhorse Publishing

Skyhorse Publishing books may be purchased in bulk at special discounts for
sales promotion, corporate gifts, fund-raising, or educational purposes. Special
editions can also be created to specifications. For details, contact the Special
Sales Department, Skyhorse Publishing, 307 West 36th Street, 11th Floor,
New York, NY 10018 or info@skyhorsepublishing.com.

Skyhorse® and Skyhorse Publishing® is a registered trademark
of Skyhorse Publishing, Inc.®, a Delaware corporation.

Visit our website at www.skyhorsepublishing.com

10 9 8 7 6 5 4 3

Library of Congress Cataloging-in-Publication Data is available
on file.

Cover design by Tom Lau

Images used under license from Shutterstock.com unless otherwise noted.

ISBN: 978-1-5107-0542-5
Ebook ISBN: 978-1-5107-0543-2

Printed in China

Contents

Disclaimer...1

Safety Warning...3

About the Author 4

Introduction..5

What This Book is Not About..7

Don't Let This Book Overwhelm You....................................9

An Important Note about Acquiring Knowledge
      and Skills...10

A Very Important Aspect of Your
      Emergency Preparedness Planning..............................12

Location, Location, Location!..15

A Brief Word about the Organization of This Book.........17

My List of 235 Items You Can't Be Without.....................18

Sign Up for Free Weekly Updates
      from Preppers Illustrated 154

Please Follow Me on Social Media!....................................155

Don't Be a Stranger!..156

Disclaimer

The purpose of this book is to help people with their emergency preparedness planning. It's the goal of the author to bring to light several items that preppers might accidentally overlook and forget to store with their emergency supplies. While this book contains information about numerous items that preppers "might" want to stockpile, it's important to understand that *it is not all-inclusive,* nor is it meant to be.

It's entirely possible the author may not have mentioned certain items you might need in an emergency situation. The author hopes this book will help you by pointing out some items you might have overlooked in your emergency preparedness planning, but you alone are ultimately responsible for ensuring that you store all the items you and your family will need to survive in an emergency.

The author has tried to provide the most accurate information she can in this book and believes that the information provided herein was correct at the time this book was written.

Any trademarks mentioned in this book are included for editorial purposes only. These trademarks are the property of their respective owners.

The information contained in this book is intended for informational purposes only. The author claims no liability for the use or misuse of anything you might read in it.

Safety Warning

Keep in mind that some items in this book may pose safety hazards. The author has tried to provide safety warnings where appropriate, but ultimately it's *your responsibility* to evaluate any items you choose to store with your emergency supplies to determine if handling or using them requires any special safety precautions.

Make sure you get any necessary specialized training prior to using any of the items mentioned in this book. Also, be sure to always follow any applicable safety procedures and/or wear appropriate safety gear when using or handling potentially hazardous items.

Do not allow children or people who aren't mentally or physically capable of safely handling or using any items in this book access to them. If you choose to allow anyone to handle emergency preparedness items that could be hazardous, you are doing so at your own risk.

Some items listed in this book are intended for rendering first aid in an emergency. It's crucial that the person performing any first aid procedures has proper training from a qualified instructor. Additionally, whenever possible, seek professional medical attention when necessary.

About the Author

Patty Hahne is the author of preppersillustrated.com which is an online magazine designed to help people with their emergency preparedness needs. She is also the author of *The Doomsday Prepping Crash Course—The Ultimate Prepper's Guide to Getting Prepared When You're on a Tight Budget*.

That book was based on two previous eBooks by Patty Hahne: *Doomsday Prepping Crash Course: The Ultimate Preppers Guide to Getting Prepared When You're on a Tight Budget* and *Build the Ideal Bug Out Bag: The Ultimate Guide to Preparing a 72 Hour Survival Kit for Surviving Comfortably*. Both titles are available on Amazon.com.

Introduction

One thing all preppers have in common is that they feel a deep sense of urgency when it comes to preparing for emergencies. Most preppers go to great lengths to stockpile everything they think they might possibly need in a doomsday scenario, but preppers are only human. This means it is entirely possible, and even likely, that there may be some items they have overlooked and/or neglected to store with their emergency preparedness supplies.

This book contains 235 items preppers *might* not have thought about storing. If you're already a prepper, it's highly likely that many of the items in this book are already stored safely away at your home, but some items mentioned in this book might not be in your stockpile yet. Keep in mind that every prepper is different, which means that one prepper's emergency preparedness needs might be completely different than another's.

You might have already taken steps to store many of the items mentioned in this book while another prepper, who is just beginning to prep, might find several items they hadn't even considered storing.

If you find items mentioned in this book you have already stored, great! Simply skip those items and move along to the next one in the list. Please don't be offended if this book lists items you have already stockpiled. Just pat yourself on the back because you've already taken the steps to store items that someone else may have overlooked. Hopefully, while reading this book, you'll discover several items you will decide to add to your stockpile of emergency supplies.

You'll notice that some items on the list in this book will have detailed explanations about why I believe it is important to include them in a prepper's emergency preparedness planning. Others won't, because no explanation is really necessary.

What This Book
is Not About

There have been many books written about preparing for doomsday or other natural disasters we might face at some point in the future. Most of these books contain the basic items preppers usually store, such as food, water, and medical supplies.

This book will not cover all the items you should have in your food storage or medical supply kit, but it will hopefully cover some things you might not have considered when it comes to storing emergency preparedness supplies.

If you're looking for a book that will hold your hand and tell you exactly how many pounds of rice and beans you should be storing, this book probably isn't for you. If, on the other hand, you're looking for a book that might help make you aware of certain items you may have overlooked in your emergency preparedness planning, it should be right up your alley.

My goal with this book is to *get you thinking and to stimulate your creative juices*. By reading it, you'll hopefully think of other items you would like to store, many of which may not even be listed in this book. I hope that reading this book will be an exercise in brainstorming for you, and that you'll be able to take what you read in it and become an even more prepared prepper.

Don't Let This Book Overwhelm You

As you can tell by the title of this book, this list is pretty extensive. Keep in mind that prepping is a process. No one goes to the store one time and purchases everything they will need to survive during a natural disaster or a doomsday scenario.

As you read through this list, you will see plenty of items you may want to include with your stockpile of emergency supplies. It's important not to let yourself become overwhelmed if you realize that you don't have some of these items already stored.

Think of this list as sort of a checklist of supplies you *may want* to accumulate *over time*. It stands to reason that some items, such as food, water, and shelter are essential for survival so you will have to prioritize which items you want to store first. After all, it won't do you much good to have a sewing kit if you don't have anything stored to eat or drink.

Once you have the essentials stored, you can start working your way through this list and begin storing additional items you think will help you survive during a natural disaster or major emergency.

An Important Note about Acquiring Knowledge and Skills

You'll notice as you read through this book that many of the items listed will require specialized skills and/or knowledge in order to be able to use them properly. For example, this book will contain suggestions about certain tools you might want to have on hand.

Sure, it's not very difficult to cook a pot of rice and beans for dinner, but when equipment you are counting on to survive with during a crisis breaks down, you'll need to know how to do the repairs yourself. In addition to tools, this will require knowledge and skills.

Of course, we hope that a doomsday scenario that lasts for an extended period of time never occurs, but as preppers, most of us prepare as if that day will in fact come at some point in time. When, and if this happens, the knowledge and skills you have acquired or developed prior to the catastrophe that causes the doomsday scenario will become invaluable to you.

In a real survival situation, it's very possible that the best gear you can have is right between your ears—your brain! The more knowledge you have, the better your chances of surviving will be. It's extremely important to understand and embrace the concept that developing knowledge and skills is just as important as stockpiling supplies.

Many situations you might find yourself in will require you to improvise and draw upon skills you have acquired prior to the emergency. Being able to think on your feet and utilize the knowledge and skills you have, should make the process of surviving easier.

A Very Important Aspect of Your Emergency Preparedness Planning

The first thing I suggest you do won't cost you a single penny, but it will be invaluable to you when it comes to planning your emergency preparedness strategies and organizing your stockpile of supplies.

If you haven't already done so, and before you acquire any more supplies, I highly recommend you make the time to take a thorough inventory of any and all emergency supplies you already have. If you've been prepping for quite some time, there's a very high likelihood you have supplies you may have forgotten all about.

Along with taking an inventory of the supplies you already have, you should make detailed notes about exactly where they are stored. I suggest you establish some sort of categorizing and mapping system so you can easily find items when you need them.

You should also include the date you purchased each particular item on your inventory list. Some items you store won't have expiration dates, but a lot of them will. Having a well-organized inventory of your supplies will not only make it easier to find particular items during an emergency, it will also help you evaluate exactly how close you are toward achieving your prepping goals.

As you take this inventory, you may find items you'll have to dispose of and replace because they've passed their expiration dates. One of the biggest mistakes preppers can make is to *assume* that they are prepared for emergencies because they remember stockpiling something at one point in time.

If you stored a particular perishable item ten years ago, there is a very high likelihood that it needs to be disposed of and replaced. You may have a false sense of security because you remember storing a particular item that won't be of any use to you in a survival situation because it's so old now.

Once you've taken an accurate inventory and categorized everything in your emergency stockpile, you'll be in a much better position to decide what you should purchase and/or store next. Your inventory list will also help as you read through this book to decide which items you may want to add to your emergency stockpile and which items you can skip over because you already have them.

For those of you who would like to keep an inventory on your computer, creating a simple spreadsheet can really help to organize your inventory list. This option is my personal favorite because by having it stored in a spreadsheet, I can easily add to, or remove from it, as I need to. I can also easily sort the perishable items by the dates that they were stored or by their expiration dates.

This is really helpful when it comes to knowing which items need to be used and replaced before they expire and are no longer of any use to my family. In addition to being able to edit the spreadsheet, I can print it so I can have a hard copy in the event of a prolonged power outage.

Location, Location, Location!

When it comes to buying a home or starting a business, you've probably heard the age-old expression "location, location, location." This is also very true when it comes to storing emergency preparedness supplies.

For example, if you live in a flood zone and you have a basement in your home, it probably wouldn't be very wise to store your food storage and other emergency preparedness supplies there. A natural disaster that results in a major flood could wipe out your entire stockpile of supplies in a matter of minutes.

Many people keep their emergency supplies in their garage, but this can also pose problems. Garages aren't typically climate-controlled, which means they could get very hot in the summer and very cold in the winter. If you have hundreds of quarts of vegetables in regular glass jars and they all freeze during the winter, you could lose them during one frigid night. On the other end of the spectrum, extreme heat may decrease the shelf life of certain items you have stored.

The bottom line is that you will be going to great lengths to build up your supply of emergency supplies so it's a worthwhile endeavor to take measures to ensure you are storing them under the best conditions possible.

A Brief Word about the Organization of This Book

It's important to understand that the items are not listed in any particular order of importance. An item you think should be listed near the top of the list, another person may think should be listed near the bottom.

My List of 235 Items
You Can't Be Without

Without further ado, let's get started.

1.   **Quality Shelving:** If you're going to all the trouble
     and expense of storing emergency supplies, it's a good
     idea to invest in quality shelving. Whether you build
     your own, or purchase commercially available shelving,
     the main idea is to make sure that it is sturdy enough
     to withstand the weight of the items you'll be placing
     on it.

Special thought and consideration should go into the design or selection of your shelving. Ideally, it will be designed so that you have easy access to the items you have stored on it. An added bonus would be to have a method of mapping out the shelves. For example, if you look at your inventory list of emergency supplies and see that a particular item is stored at C-3-11, this could mean you have assigned the shelf the letter "C", "3" is the third shelf from the bottom, and the item is 11 sections from the left on the shelf.

You can use whatever method of mapping out your shelves you want. The idea behind this strategy is to develop an easy way to locate the items you need quickly. Having all your supplies thrown in a big pile in the corner of your garage or basement is a really bad idea because you may not be able to find a particular item when you need it.

2. **Thread:** You never know when you're going to have to mend some articles of clothing or survival gear. You should have several spools of thread on hand. Keep in mind that not all emergencies will last forever.

It's entirely possible you might have to live without some of the normal conveniences of life for a while and then things may return to normal. If you only have purple thread to mend your clothes you may find

 yourself wanting to throw away your favorite orange shirt when society gets back to normal and your shirt still has a bunch of purple seams. a bunch of purple seams.

It's also a good idea to have several thicknesses of thread on hand. After all, it wouldn't make much sense to use the same thickness of thread to repair a hole in your socks as it would to repair a broken strap on your backpack. If you have gear that is made out of leather, you may want to purchase some special waxed thread that is specifically designed for repairing it.

3. **Sewing Needles:** It stands to reason that if you're going to have thread on hand for making repairs to clothing and gear, you should have a wide assortment of various types and sizes of sewing needles as well.

   It would probably be a good idea to also purchase some curved sewing needles. These needles can come in very handy when making repairs in difficult to reach areas. As mentioned in the previous paragraph, not all repairs call for the same thickness of thread. Make sure the sewing needles you store have different sizes of eyes to accommodate the different thicknesses of threads you are storing.

Keeping in mind that you may have to exert a considerable amount of pressure to get the needle to poke through thick material, having heavy duty needles on hand would probably also be a good idea. Otherwise, you're just going to end up breaking them.

4. **Scissors:** It would probably be a good idea to have a variety of different types of scissors on hand as well. While some scissors are designed for cutting things like cloth, others are designed very robustly and can cut through material as thick as sheet metal.

Another reason it's a good idea to have several pairs of scissors on hand is that if one pair becomes dull, you'll have another pair to use as a backup. Scissors *can* be sharpened, but they are very difficult to sharpen properly. It's better to have a few backup pairs on hand in the event that your favorite pair becomes dull than to have to try to sharpen them.

5. **Patterns for Sewing:** If you're handy with a needle and thread, you might be able to make clothing for your family members. Having an assortment of sewing patterns on hand could come in very handy. Make sure you have the appropriate sizes of patterns for all your family members so that when their shirts or pants wear out, you can make replacements for them.

6. **Awl:** If you're not familiar with this handy tool, let me describe it for you. An awl is basically a very strong, sharp needle with a wooden handle designed for poking holes in thick material such as leather.

If you find yourself having to repair leather goods, you may discover that it's quite difficult to push a needle through the thick leather. This is where an awl comes in very handy. You can use the sharp point of the awl to poke holes in the leather so you can more easily pass a needle and thread through them to make the necessary repairs.

7. **Safety Pins:** This is perhaps one of the most useful things to keep in your sewing kit. Depending on the circumstances you find yourself in, you may not have enough time to stop and properly mend your clothing.

If you have a variety of sizes of safety pins on hand, you can make quick repairs in the field. Later, when

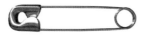

you have enough time to do the repair properly, you simply remove the safety pin and store it away so it can be used again in the future.

Safety pins are also helpful if you have an infant in diapers. Depending on how long you have to survive in a doomsday scenario, you may find that your supply of disposable diapers will eventually run out. Having a good supply of safety pins can be very important for diapering a young child If you happen to use cloth diapers as a backup. If you use safety pins for diapering a child, make sure they are child-safe and designed for that purpose.

Another very handy use for safety pins is when you have the clasp break off of a zipper. Zippers can be extremely convenient, but if you lose the clasp, it can be difficult, if not impossible, to zip them up or down.

8. **Spare Fabric:** If you're going to store supplies to make repairs on clothing, it makes sense you should have some spare pieces of material stored away as well. This is another item that doesn't have to cost you anything at all. You can simply save material from clothing you intend to throw out. You can also ask your friends and neighbors to save their old clothing so you can cut it up to store away with your emergency supplies. You'll probably find that they'll be more than happy to accommodate you.

Keeping in mind that we don't know how long a doomsday scenario might last, you may find yourself in a situation where you need to make new clothing items for your family members. In addition to storing scraps of fabric you have cut from old items, you might want to have a stockpile of new fabric you can use to make new clothing.

Pants may be more likely to wear out than shirts so it would probably be a good idea to keep a supply of denim on hand. This will make it possible for you to make new jeans for your family members should the need arise.

9. **Straight Pins:** This is an item that doesn't take up much room at all. If you are going to be sewing clothing, having a supply of straight pins available will certainly prove to be useful.

10. **Buttons:** This is another item that is very easy to stockpile. Buttons are small which means they don't take up much space, but you'll be really glad you have a backup supply of them if you happen to lose a button on your shirt or jeans.

    Here's a handy tip. The next time you cut up an old shirt or pair of pants, cut the buttons off instead of disposing of them. Store the buttons with your emergency supplies and, before you know it, you'll have plenty of them put aside for a rainy day.

11. **Zippers:** This is an item that's very easy to forget. After all, we don't spend much time thinking about zippers until one breaks. If you've ever had the zipper on your pants break, you realize what an inconvenience it can be. You can also ask your friends and family members to save their old, worn-out clothing so you can "harvest" the old zippers.

Again, this is an item you don't have to go down to the store and buy. Simply take a few minutes and remove the old zippers from items of clothing you are cutting up. Over time, you'll be amazed at how many zippers you are able to accumulate!

Another great idea is to shop at secondhand stores or yard sales for old items of clothing that have functioning zippers on them. It doesn't matter what condition the clothing is in either because you're simply going to remove the zipper to save it.

12. **Velcro®:** This is an absolutely amazing invention. It can be used on everything from clothing to backpacks. You can purchase Velcro® that is designed to be sewn in or you can purchase the kind that has a double-sided adhesive backing to it. It might be a good idea to have a bit of both types on hand.

Something else you may not know is that you can purchase heavy duty Velcro® that is much stronger than the type you might be accustomed to. The heavy duty variety could be very useful for tasks that the regular variety isn't strong enough for.

13. **Zip Ties:** These little items are extremely useful for a variety of purposes. Also known as "cable ties," they can be used for so many purposes in a survival situation that it's difficult to even begin to name them all.

One thing worth mentioning is that if you decide to store this particular type of item, you may want to

purchase them in a variety of sizes. Having access to multiple sizes of zip ties will make this versatile item even more useful to you.

Something else you might not realize is that you can purchase zip ties that can be loosened and used over again and again. In most cases, once you tighten a zip tie, you have to cut it to remove it. The reusable type might be better to store because they aren't one-time-use items.

14. **Rags:** This is one item that all preppers should have on hand and they're not expensive to stockpile either. As a matter of fact, there's no reason that rags should have to cost you anything at all. The next time you get ready to throw away an old shirt or a pair of worn out pants, take five minutes and cut the material into rag-size pieces you can use for a variety of survival purposes.

You can also have your friends or family members save old clothing for you that you can cut up for rags. Other good sources for rags are yard sales and thrift stores. There are so many sources for rag material that you should be able to accumulate a large amount quite easily.

15. **Knitting Needles:** If you're handy with knitting needles, you can use these little gadgets to make

everything from sweaters to stocking caps for those long, cold winter days. Not only do they have a utilitarian purpose, they can also help you pass the time.

In a doomsday scenario, you may not have access to electricity and you might find that you'll become quite bored. This is the perfect time to break out the old knitting needles and start working on a project.

16. **Crochet Hooks:** If you know how to crochet and you have some crochet hooks, you can make a wide variety of useful items. A couple that come to mind are afghan blankets and scarves. This is another item that can help alleviate boredom while you are trying to pass the time after a natural disaster or some other type of doomsday scenario.

17. **Yarn:** If you are going to keep some knitting needles and crochet hooks stored away, it makes sense that you should have a collection of yarn stored away as well. Might I suggest that you purchase wool yarn? If you are making things like stocking hats and scarves, wool yarn would be a good material to make them out of because it has excellent insulating properties.

18. **Engine Oil:** You should have enough oil on hand that is the appropriate type for all your vehicles. As a matter of fact, you should have spare oil on hand for any power equipment that has an internal combustion engine.

Oil is one thing an engine cannot do without. If your engine runs too low on oil and you don't have any replacement oil, you might as well not have an engine at all because it will quickly be destroyed without proper lubrication.

19. **Grease:** All preppers should have some grease on hand. You never know when you'll need to lubricate something. Whether it's a part on your vehicle or a pivot point on a garden tool, having grease available could come in very handy. After all, there are certain things that simply cannot function unless they are properly lubricated.

It might be a good idea to have two types of grease stored up. The first is the kind that comes in a container that you apply with your fingers. This could be useful for things like repacking the grease in wheel

bearings. The other type of grease to have on hand is the kind that comes in a tube that fits inside a hand powered grease pump. These devices have a special fitting on the end designed to attach to what are called "zerk" fittings. You'll find zerk fittings on many of the major lubrication points for your vehicles, as well as on many lubrication points for power equipment.

20. **Fuel Siphon:** If you run short on gasoline for your emergency generator, you may find that you'll need to siphon it from one of your vehicles. A fuel siphon that has a built-in, hand-powered pump can be used to transfer fuel from your vehicle's tank to a gas can.

    Warning: You should never siphon fuel by sucking on the end of a hose with your mouth because it can pose a significant health hazard. A siphon that has a built-in, hand-powered pump is a much better tool for performing this chore.

21. **Gas Cans in a Variety of Sizes:** As preppers, we try to do all we can to prepare for whatever might come our way, but the truth of the matter is we really don't have any idea what will actually happen.

    You may find yourself in a situation where people have abandoned their vehicles permanently. For example, imagine a situation where an EMP were to disable thousands upon thousands of vehicles. In a situation like this, the streets and highways would probably be littered with disabled vehicles that all have some gasoline in their tanks.

    I'm certainly not suggesting you steal from anyone or break any laws for that matter. Having said that, in a major, prolonged doomsday scenario where a massive number of vehicles are *permanently* abandoned, some of you might decide to siphon gasoline from their tanks to power your backup generators. Without a supply of gas cans, you won't have any way of safely transporting the gasoline you are able to scavenge back to your camp or home.

One thing that's worth keeping in mind is that if all you have are five-gallon gas cans, it could be quite physically demanding to carry them when they are full back to your camp or home. This is why it might be a good idea to have several sizes of gas cans at your disposal. Carrying a one-gallon can would be much less physically demanding than carrying a five-gallon can over a long distance.

Here's another thing to think about. If you have several one gallon cans and you venture out to scavenge for gasoline with multiple people in your group, each person may be able to carry a gallon of gasoline back to your home or camp. The old expression that goes, "many hands make light work" also holds true for carrying supplies over any significant distance.

22. **Liquid Gasket Maker:** You never know when you'll have to make repairs on your vehicles or power equipment. Gaskets are one of those things you don't think about until one isn't holding a seal properly.

It would probably be a good idea to store several tubes of liquid gasket maker so that you can do field repairs on your engines. This may not be the ideal way to repair a blown gasket, but if you don't have a spare gasket on hand, it may be your only option.

If you've never used this type of product before, I should point out that they make different formulations for various temperature ratings. If you only have the type designed for low temperatures and you need to make a gasket for a part of your engine that gets really hot, you'll be out of luck as it just won't be up to the task. With this in mind, I suggest that you store a variety of different types.

23. **Starting Fluid:** Sometimes you might come up against stubborn engines that just won't start. This is especially true if the engine hasn't been run for quite some time. Sometimes a couple of quick squirts of starting fluid can help a stubborn engine fire up. It can also be useful when troubleshooting an engine that is difficult to get started.

   Warning: Be sure to follow the directions on the can precisely to make sure that you don't start a fire when using this product. Using too much starting fluid, or using it improperly, can be dangerous! Additionally, there may be certain types of engines that the manufacturer advises against using starting fluid in.

24. **Fuses:** All vehicles require fuses to protect their sensitive electronic components. If you blow a fuse and you don't have a spare, you're going to be out of

luck. This isn't one of those things you can backwards engineer out of baling wire and duct tape.

You should have a wide assortment of various types of fuses stored. Keep in mind that some vehicles use dif-ferent types and sizes of fuses. Also, you should only replace a blown fuse with one that is the correct size, type, and amp rating. Keep a supply of fuses on hand for each of your vehicles.

Don't forget about things like your power equipment either. Your emergency generator may use fuses. Your tractor may use fuses. Your power inverter may use fuses. The list could go on and on so take an inventory of all your items that require them to make sure you have the proper replacement fuses stockpiled.

25. **Multimeter:** This is a handy and fairly inexpensive tool that can be used to diagnose a number of electrical problems if you know what you're doing. It can even test to see what the voltages are in batteries, which could come in extremely handy. If you find yourself having to scavenge for batteries, having a multimeter to use will let you quickly know whether the battery has a charge or not.

A multimeter can also tell you whether or not you have a bad wire. It can also be used to test various electrical components to determine whether or not they are still usable.

Warning: *Testing electrical components can pose the risk of electrical shock and should only be done by someone who is qualified and properly trained to do so. Additionally, always make sure you follow any applicable safety procedures while testing electrical components.*

26. **Magnets:** There are so many uses for magnets that it's hard to list them all. One very good use for a magnet is to help find lost nuts or bolts you may have dropped in the gravel while you were working on a piece of equip-  ment. This happens all the time and a good powerful magnet may help you find it in no time at all.

You can also buy a handy device that has a telescoping or flexible shaft with a strong magnet on the end of it. This tool can be used to retrieve nuts or bolts you may have dropped while working under the hood of a vehicle. Often you can't get your hands in the tight crevices where nuts and bolts end up landing, so this tool can really save your bacon.

27. **Spare Belts for Vehicles:** All vehicles require some belts to run things like alternators, water pumps, air conditioning compressors, and power steering pumps. If you break an essential belt and you don't have a replacement, your vehicle will be useless to you.

It would be a good idea to take an inventory of your vehicles and any power equipment that requires their use. Make sure you have a spare belt or two on hand for all these devices.

28. **Carburetor Cleaner:** Old carburetors can some-times become clogged up with a gummy sludge. You may find that you'll have to do an in-the-field repair to clean out a carburetor.

    Carburetor cleaner comes in two forms. It comes in a pressurized can that has a small tube you insert in the nozzle. This makes it possible to direct a concentrated stream into the tiny orifices of the carburetor that you might be working on.

    It also comes in a non-pressurized can so you can pour it in a container and soak the carburetor that you are working on. It might be a good idea to have a few cans of both types of carburetor cleaner stockpiled. Without this, it might be impossible to get the carburetor you are working on functioning properly again.

    Here's a tip. Don't expose rubber O-rings, seals, or plastic components of your carburetor to this product as it may permanently damage them.

    Warning: Always wear safety glasses and chemical-resistant rubber gloves when working with carburetor cleaner.

29. **Carburetor Kits:** A carburetor kit basically con-tains all the small components that are inside of a

carburetor that make it function properly—gaskets, O-rings, needle seats, and more.

Ideally, you'll do a good job of keeping your engines serviced so that the carburetor doesn't need to be rebuilt. But, if your carburetor does happen to fail, having a carburetor kit on hand will help ensure that you have the necessary supplies to get your engine running properly again.

Most vehicles these days are fuel-injected so this doesn't apply to a lot of modern cars or trucks, but it does apply to power equipment, such as emergency generators. I suggest you keep appropriate carburetor kits on hand for your emergency generator and any other power equipment you plan to rely on during a doomsday scenario.

30. **Spare Spark Plugs:** You should keep spare spark plugs on hand for your vehicles, as well as for your emergency generator. When it comes to spark plugs, it's very simple—if the spark plug doesn't provide the correct intensity of spark, your engine won't run or it won't run well.

    Keep in mind that this isn't a one-size-fits-all type of thing. Various engines use different sizes of spark plugs so make sure you keep the proper sizes and types stored for all your equipment.

Here's a handy tip. Use a permanent marker and write the name of the engine that the particular spark plug(s) are intended for use in on their boxes. This way, you'll be more likely to put the correct spark plug(s) in the engine that you might be working on.

31. **Spark Plug Gapping Tool:** This is a small and inexpensive tool that only costs about two dollars. Although it's small and inexpensive, it's essential to have. When you replace the spark plugs in your engine, this tool is used to ensure that the proper gap is set on the spark plugs.

Various engines require that spark plug gaps be set to different specifications. This isn't one of those things you can simply guess at and you can't take a spark plug out of the box and expect it to perform perfectly in your engine without properly gapping it first.

I should point out that in *some cases* you may be able to purchase spark plugs that are supposed to be pre-gapped from the factory. If you buy these types of plugs, it's still a good idea to manually check them with your gapping tool to make sure they were actually gapped to the correct specifications.

32. **Spare Hoses:** All vehicles require certain sizes and types of hoses to run properly. For example, your car

will have radiator hoses, heater hoses, and fuel lines. If one of these hoses develops a leak, it will need to be replaced. This isn't the type of thing you can fix with electrical tape, duct tape, or silicone.

Your generator will also have a fuel line that connects the fuel tank to the carburetor. If this develops a leak, you'll definitely want to have a spare fuel line on hand so you can make the necessary repair.

33. **Hose Clamps:** Keep in mind that most hoses are fastened with metal hose clamps of some kind. In addition to having spare hoses stored, you should make sure you have the proper hose clamps to do the repair in the event that one of the clamps breaks or becomes damaged while you are removing it.

34. **Penetrating Oil:** Often, when you are trying to remove a nut or a bolt, you'll find that it is quite difficult, if not impossible to turn. A good quality penetrating oil that is specifically designed to help break free the rust and debris that might be preventing you from being able to turn a stuck nut or bolt can be extremely helpful in a situation like this.

Keep in mind that this type of a product usually works best if you spray it on the stubborn nut or bolt and let it sit for quite some time. Letting it have enough time to do its job can make the difference between you being able to remove the stuck fastener or stripping or even breaking the bolt off completely. Sometimes it can be helpful to spray a stream of penetrating oil on the particular stuck fastener every couple of hours while you're waiting for it to do its job.

35. **Left-Handed Drill Bits:** If the use of penetrating oil doesn't make it possible for you to remove the bolt and it actually breaks, you can sometimes remove it using left-handed drill bits.

Traditional drill bits are designed to drill a hole when they are spun in a clockwise direction. Left-handed drill bits are designed to drill a hole when they are spun in a counterclockwise direction. This is why they can sometimes be helpful in removing a broken bolt. You've probably heard the age-old expression, "righty tighty, lefty loosey." This is an easy way of remembering that most bolts or nuts get tight when you turn them to the right and they loosen or come out when you turn them to the left.

If you are working on something and the bolt head breaks off and it's flush with the surface of the equipment you're working on, you can sometimes remove it by using a center punch and a hammer to create a small divot in the center of the broken bolt. Then, using an electric drill with a left-handed drill bit that is *smaller* than the diameter of the broken bolt, you slowly begin to drill out the center. What you are hoping will happen is that the drill bit will actually bite into the bolt as the drill is spinning it and extract the broken bolt as if you were turning it with a wrench. Remember to use your drill at a slow speed as you aren't really trying to drill a hole in the bolt. The goal is for the drill bit to start to drill a hole and then grab hold of the bolt and slowly extract it. If your drill is spinning at a high RPM, you are more likely to simply drill a hole in the bolt. If you choose to try this method, be very careful. If you use too much force with your drill once the bit grabs hold, you could end up breaking the drill bit and ultimately making your problem worse.

36. **Screw Extractors:** If neither the use of penetrating oil nor the left-handed drill bit works to extract a broken bolt, you can sometimes get them out using a specialty tool called a "screw extractor."

These tools look similar to drill bits except they are usually tapered. They are used in a similar way that left-handed drill bits are used. You first have to center punch the broken bolt and then you have to drill out the center of the bolt using a drill bit that is smaller than the diameter of the bolt you are trying to remove.

Keep in mind that you don't want to damage the threads of the part that the bolt is screwed into so you want to make sure that the drill bit you use isn't so large it will remove or damage the threads as you are drilling. After you have drilled a hole in the center, you use the screw extractor that has threads that are designed to bite into the bolt as you turn it counter-clockwise. I should point out that, at least in the United

States, most fasteners have threads that enable the bolt or nut to tighten when turned clockwise and loosen when turned counterclockwise. That being said, in some rare circumstances, the bolt or nut may actually have what are known as "reverse threads." This means that they get tight when turned counterclockwise and loose when turned clockwise. For example, I believe that one of my husband's power saws has a reverse thread bolt that holds the blade on. While this is the exception to the rule, it's important to know that you could encounter a fastener with reverse threads in some rare cases.

37. **Tap & Die Set:** If all else fails and you aren't able to remove the broken bolt using any of the methods described above, you may have to resort to completely drilling out the old bolt. If this happens, it will destroy the threads and you'll need some way of rethreading the hole.

This is where the use of a tap and die set comes in. A "tap" is a specially designed tool that is used for cutting or repairing threads in a hole that is drilled into a metal surface. A tap can also often be used for cleaning up or repairing damaged threads in a nut. A "die" is similar to a tap with the exception that it is designed to cut or repair threads on a bolt.

This tool can be invaluable if you happen to damage or cross-thread a bolt as you are attempting to screw it into a threaded hole or you are trying to put a nut on it. With the use of a die, you may be able to repair the damaged threads so that the bolt can be properly inserted into a threaded hole or have a nut properly threaded onto it.

Something that could help make this process go more smoothly is to use cutting oil to lubricate the hole or bolt. This oil is specially designed to help the tap or die cut the metal more easily and precisely.

38. **Jumper Cables:** We live in a day and age where emergency roadside service is just a cell phone call away. Because of these types of modern conveniences, many people don't carry jumper cables in their vehicles anymore. If you find yourself with a dead battery, you aren't going to be able to make a phone call to an emergency roadside service for a quick jump start.

    One might think that choosing a set of jumper cables would be quite simple, but there is something very important to keep in mind when it comes to purchasing them. The main thing to remember is that you want to purchase jumper cables that have a very heavy gauge of wire. The thicker the wire, the more electricity or "current" will be able to flow from the charging vehicle's battery to your dead battery.

    If you have an inexpensive set of cables with thin wires or cheap clamps, you may find that you won't be able to jump start your battery at all, depending on how low the voltage is. When it comes to purchasing jumper cables that you plan on using in a doomsday type scenario, spend a little bit of extra money and buy cables with very thick wires and very good clamps on the ends.

Of course, make sure you don't get your wires crossed and that you follow the manufacturer's recommended procedures whenever jump-starting a vehicle.

39. **Service Manuals:** If a doomsday scenario lasts very long, you'll find that you need to be your own mechanic. Having the proper service manuals on hand for your vehicles, power equipment, and emergency generators will be essential.

    Keep in mind that when it comes to things like emergency generators, the generator and the engine for the generator often have two different service manuals. Make sure you have both the service manual for the generator *and* the engine on hand. This will help you make the proper repairs should you find yourself in a situation where your generator isn't functioning properly.

40. **Spare Engine-Starting Pull Cord:** Virtually all small to mid-sized emergency generators will come with a pull-start system. Some will come with electric starters but you can't always rely on them. Over time,

the repetitive motion of pulling on the cord to start a generator may cause the cord to fray and break. If you have some spare starting cord on hand, you can make the repair and you'll be able to start your engine once again. If you don't, you may find that your generator will be absolutely useless to you since you'll have no way to start it.

41. **Distilled Water:** This is water that has been put through a process that removes any impurities. In many cases, things like minerals, heavy metals, and other contaminants are removed during the distillation process. Distilled water has a couple of good uses. One is that if you are adding water to your vehicle's radiator, you will want to use distilled water. Using regular tap water that contains minerals may cause problems with your engine's cooling system.

Another very common use for distilled water is for those people who require a CPAP or BiPAP machine to sleep at night. Using regular tap water in the humidifier reservoir isn't advised so you'll be glad you thought ahead and stored some distilled water if you rely on one of these machines.

You can also make your own distilled water using simple equipment that you probably already have around your house. Here's a URL for a document you can download from FEMA that shows how to distill water using common household supplies: www.fema.gov/pdf/library/f&web.pdf.

42. **Plunger:** Everyone should have a basic plunger on hand. Sometimes minor clogs in toilets and sink drains can be quickly cleared with a plunger. There are two kinds you might want to consider purchasing. The first is the old-fashioned rubber plunger with a wooden handle. This type of plunger has served many households well over the years.

The second, a more modern version of the plunger is made from plastic and has a flexible, plastic accordion-shaped plunger end that is capable of delivering much more pressure down the drain than a standard rubber plunger.

43. **Closet Auger:** The closet auger is also commonly referred to as a "drain snake." It's an inexpensive, yet handy device that can often be used to unclog stubborn toilets and drains.

Remember, if civilized society breaks down, you're not going to be able to call your local plumber to come unclog your drains for you. This device can sometimes be much more useful than a common plunger because it will actually feed its way through the passageways of your toilet and it should remove any blockages that might be in them.

If you live in a city, you may not have the luxury of being able to flush your toilet, but if you live in the country and you get your water from a well and you have some way of actually pumping water from it, your toilets should still function fine. That is, unless they get clogged up and you don't have this tool to unclog them. It's not a difficult device to use and it could really come in quite handy for you someday. If you make the investment in this tool, you'll probably find yourself using it even if we never experience a doomsday scenario.

44. **Hand Pump for Your Well:** If you live in the country and you get your water from a well, you probably realize that without electricity, there won't be any water flowing from your faucets. Fortunately, you can purchase hand pumps designed to be attached to a well head that can be used for pumping water

from a well. This is a great item to have because it means you will have access to water even if the electric grid goes down.

Be sure you purchase one designed to pump water from the actual depth of the water level in your well. You should also make sure you don't just buy one of these devices and store it away with your emergency preparedness items. It will require some special installation procedures and may need parts you might not have on hand during a natural disaster.

45. **Regular Liquid Household Chlorine Bleach:** This is an item that can be used for a variety of things. In addition to helping with your laundry, it can be used for disinfecting things and chlorinating water. FEMA has provided a document you can refer to if you want to learn how they recommend using this item for treating water during emergency situations. You should download, print it out, and keep it on hand so you will have it for future reference. Here's the URL to the document: www.fema.gov/pdf/library/f&web.pdf.

Here is a direct quote from the FEMA document referred to above about the type of bleach they recommend using: "*Use only regular household liquid bleach that contains 5.25 to 6.0 percent sodium hypochlorite. Do not use scented bleaches, colorsafe bleaches, or bleaches with added cleaners. Because the potency of bleach diminishes with time, use bleach from a newly opened or unopened bottle.*" Because FEMA says you should only use bleach from newly opened or unopened containers, it might be a good idea to store many small bottles of bleach instead of one or two large bottles. This way, you'll have a good supply of unopened bottles available should you need them.

Warning: As with all chemicals, this item should be kept out of the hands of children or those who aren't able to handle it safely.

46. **Empty Two-Liter Soda Bottles:** The document from FEMA that I referred to above contains infor-

mation about how you can use empty two-liter plastic soda bottles for storing water. In addition to being able to store water in these bottles, they make handy containers that can be used for a variety of survival purposes.

47. **Chimney Cleaning Tools:** If you plan on relying on a wood stove to heat your home or cook your food, you're going to want to have a way to clean  your chimney. Over time, a substance called creosote accumulates on the inner lining of your chimney. You should have a wire chimney brush that is the proper size for your particular chimney available to use.

One type of chimney brush cleans a chimney by attaching flexible fiberglass rods to the threaded end of a wire brush that is the appropriate size. They are each roughly four feet in length, and as you push the chimney brush further and further into your chimney, you will add a length of the fiberglass rod one section at a time. Be sure and get training on how to use this tool properly to clean your chimney before you actually need to use it.

The reason this tool is so important to have is because if creosote accumulates on the inside of your chimney walls, it's possible for it to combust and start a fire that could cause your entire house to burn down! Part of responsibly using a wood stove to heat your home is proper and regular cleaning of the chimney.

48. **Files for Sharpening Tools:** Hand tools such as axes, hatchets, splitting mauls, and machetes often require sharpening. It would be a good idea to keep a few files on hand so you can sharpen them when you need to.

You can purchase files in various sizes and degrees of coarseness. Some coarse files are designed to remove a lot of material at once, while other files with fine grooves are more suited for putting the finishing edge on your hand tools.

Be sure to purchase and attach handles for your files as well. They are much easier and safer to use with handles attached to them. Also, make sure to use caution and follow any necessary safety procedures when sharpening or handling tools.

49. **Wire Brushes:** Wire brushes can be used for all sorts of things. We just mentioned keeping files on hand for sharpening tools. They actually make a special wire brush called a "file card" that is specifically designed for cleaning out any metal shavings that might accumulate in the crevices of your files.

Wire brushes are also very handy for cleaning corrosion off of battery terminals in your vehicles. These are just a few uses for this item. The list could go on and on.

50. **Shovel with Metal Handle or Break-Resistant Fiberglass Handle:** You never know when you'll need a shovel. Whether you're digging a hole for an emergency outhouse, or you're preparing soil for planting a garden, a good shovel will be invaluable.

I don't recommend a shovel with a wooden handle because if you break it, your shovel will be useless to you. Instead, buy a high quality shovel with a sturdy metal handle or break-resistant fiberglass handle.

While we're talking about shovels, you might want to consider having a few different types on hand. For example, a shovel with a pointed tip is good for digging, while a shovel with a flat tip is better suited for scooping. Since you don't know what time of year you might find yourself faced with a survival scenario, you might also want to have a high-quality metal snow shovel on hand as well.

51. **Gardening Tools:** Depending on how long you find yourself having to survive, you may find you'll need to plant a garden to supplement your food requirements. With this in mind, you might want to make sure you have a hoe, rake, and any other gardening tools you like to use available.

52. **Watering Can:** Keep in mind you might not have water flowing from your hoses, so if you do in fact plant a garden, you'll need a way to water your plants. A watering can could help you with this chore.

It would probably be a good idea to shy away from plastic watering cans and stick to those that are made from rust-resistant metal. Plastic is just too prone to breaking.

53. **Seeds:** If you find yourself needing to grow a garden, you'll want to have a good supply of seeds on hand. Be sure you store them properly so they will be viable when you need to plant them. Follow the instructions on the seed packages for the best way to store them.

54. **Fertilizer and Pesticides:** If you plan on supplementing your nutritional needs with vegetables from your garden, you may want to have some fertilizer and/or pesticides on hand. Be sure and do research ahead of time so you'll know what type of fertilizer and/or pesticides you'll need for your particular area.

    Also, be sure you store these items properly. It probably wouldn't be a good idea to store them near your food supply. Follow the directions on the bags to determine the proper storage method for these items.

55. **Root Cellar:** Because we live in a day and age when we have many modern conveniences, not many people have root cellars anymore. For thousands of years, root cellars were used as a way of preserving vegetables that were grown during the summer so that they could be eaten throughout the winter.

A properly designed root cellar will maintain a cool temperature that should help prolong the shelf life of vegetables during the cold winter months.

This isn't really an item you would store like many of the items on this list, but it might not be a bad idea to either construct one or have one constructed by someone who is qualified to do so. If you do decide to construct your own root cellar, make sure you consult with someone who has the necessary experience to make sure it is constructed properly and safely.

56. **Greenhouse:** You may not be a gardener now, but during a prolonged doomsday scenario, you could find yourself in a situation where you have to grow your own vegetables to provide a source of food for your family.

Experienced gardeners know that a greenhouse can be very beneficial in climates that don't have long growing seasons. The idea behind a greenhouse is that it concentrates the heat from the sun to provide a warmer microclimate for vegetables to grow when the temperatures outside are too cold.

One of the main benefits of a greenhouse is that it can actually extend the growing season where you live. A risk that all gardeners take when they plant their vegetables too early in the year is that a cold snap will cause freezing temperatures that will kill the young plants.

Starting your plants in a greenhouse may help prevent this problem. Conversely, during the end of the growing season when the temperatures start to fall again, a greenhouse should help prolong the growing season which might result in your plants producing vegetables for a longer period of time before they eventually die.

Like a root cellar, this isn't an item that you store, but rather one that you construct. It's also an item that should be constructed well ahead of time so you don't find yourself scrambling to build a makeshift greenhouse while you're trying to survive during a prolonged crisis caused by some type of a natural disaster.

57. **Drip Irrigation System:** During a power grid down event, you might find yourself having to water your vegetables with a watering can. This can be a very labor-intensive chore and it may not be the most efficient way to water your plants. An alternative to watering by hand is to construct a rudimentary drip irrigation system.

Drip irrigation systems are composed of hoses with tiny holes in them that are strategically placed along the rows of your garden. The

idea behind this type of a system is that water will slowly leach into the ground over a prolonged period of time. One advantage to this type of irrigating is that the soil should stay moist over a longer period of time.

If you find yourself in a situation where you are watering your vegetables once a day with a watering can, much of the water you put on your vegetables will evaporate due to the heat of the sun beating down on them.

A makeshift drip irrigation system can be constructed with the use of a barrel of water that is higher in elevation than the garden. A hose that feeds the drip irrigation hoses can be fastened to this barrel and slowly, throughout the day, water can passively leach into the soil and water your garden for you. When constructed properly, this can be an effective way of watering a garden. An added benefit is that it can free up time for you to do other chores that need to be done.

58. **String:** String has so many uses in survival situations that there really are too many to list. Instead of listing all of the possible uses for string, let me just suggest that you store several types of it. Having a variety of types stored will help ensure that you have just the right type when you find yourself needing some.

59. **Hand Tools:** You should have a wide assortment of non-electric tools for making repairs. Power tools are

great if you have electricity, but you should assume that you won't. This way, you can still make any necessary repairs if you find yourself without electricity. You might want to include an old-fashioned hand drill and drill bits, as well as a variety of hand saws.

60. **Car Tire Repair Supplies:** You never know when you'll find yourself with a flat tire. If you've simply run over a nail with your car, you might be able to fix it yourself if you have a tire plug kit. This type of repair isn't as good as having a tire professionally repaired at a tire shop but in an  emergency, it may work for you. These kits are inexpensive and fairly simple to use.

There are also handy products such as Fix-a-Flat® that can sometimes be used to temporarily repair small punctures in tires. This product comes in a pressurized can. You simply connect the hose on it to the valve stem on your car tire and push the button. It inflates your tire while at the same time pumping sealant into the tire that is supposed to seek out the leak and seal it.

61. **Mounted Spare Tires:** Even if you have supplies to repair flat tires, there very well may be situations when

you blow a tire. If the side-wall of your tire becomes damaged, you won't be able to fix it with a tire plug kit.

With this in mind, it would probably be a good idea to have a set of spare tires that are already mounted on the appropriate sized rims for the vehicle they are intended for. After all, you most likely won't be able to find a tire repair shop to remove your blown tire and mount a replacement tire on the rim. Having a full set of tires that are already mounted on rims could save you a lot of trouble in a crisis.

62. **Bicycles:** If you find yourself in a situation where gasoline is in short supply, bicycles can be an excellent source of transportation. Mountain bikes in particular offer a wide range of gears to make pedaling easier and they are often built more robustly than traditional bicycles. Due to the fact that they tend to be sturdier in the way they are constructed, they may be less likely to break down while you are using them.

One of the main benefits of using bicycles as a form of transportation is that you'll be able to cover much more ground in a far shorter period of time than when walking. Depending upon the type of bicycle you have and how it is equipped, you may also expend less energy using it as your mode of transportation than walking or hiking.

While it may not be the most fashionable thing, wearing a good quality bicycle helmet that fits properly while you ride may help protect your head if you happen to crash. For this reason, you should always wear a bicycle helmet whenever you are riding a bike.

63. **Bicycle Trailers:** Having access to good quality bicycle trailers can be invaluable to you. Not only can you carry your gear in them,  you can also carry young children who will tire quickly if you find yourself in a situation where you have to walk over long distances.

    As an additional safety measure, you should always have any children who are riding in a bicycle trailer wear a helmet. Also, don't put children in bicycle trailers that aren't designed to transport them safely.

64. **Bicycle Saddle Bags:** If your bike is equipped with racks over the front or rear tires, you can affix bags that are commonly referred to as "saddlebags" to them. Simply put, these are bags that hang on both sides of your bike's rack so you can carry supplies in them.

You should try to balance the weight in each of the bags to make riding while you're carrying cargo a bit easier. Riding with loaded saddle bags can also affect the balance of your bike. With this in mind, make sure you use caution so you don't let the new way the bike handles cause you to lose control and crash.

65. **Bicycle Tube Repair Kit:** While we're on the topic of using bicycles as a mode of transportation, be sure to keep some bicycle tube patch kits on hand.

Make sure you buy a kit that contains the devices that are used for properly removing the bicycle tire from the rim so you can patch the tube. Some people try using screwdrivers for this task, but you can easily create more punctures in the tube if you attempt to remove the tire using screwdrivers.

Sometimes you'll end up damaging tubes beyond repair, which brings up another point. It might not be a bad idea to keep a few spare tubes with your supplies in case you get a puncture that you can't repair with a standard patch kit.

66. **Flat Tire Prevention Devices:** One of the main disadvantages of using a bicycle as your form of transpor-

tation is dealing with the inconvenience of flat tires. Fortunately, there are some products on the market that can help minimize this problem.

- You can purchase specially designed tires that have a liner made of puncture-resistant material as one possible option.
- In addition to specially designed tires, you can purchase "tire liners" that are designed to be placed between the tire and the tube to function as an added barrier of protection against thorns and other things that might cause flat tires.
- You can also purchase bicycle tubes made of thicker rubber to help minimize the number of flat tires you might get.
- You can even fill your bicycle inner tubes with a product that is known as a "tube sealant." This type of product is basically a thick liquid material designed to seek out punctures as they occur and seal them to prevent the air from leaking out of your tube.
- The last option is to use a solid bicycle tire that doesn't have a tube in it at all, although many avid cyclists don't seem to like this particular option. Some people feel they are difficult to fit onto the rims and that they don't provide as smooth a ride as pneumatic tires. Nevertheless, it is an option that eliminates the problem of flat tires.

67. **High Quality Foot Pump:** If you find yourself having to repair car or bicycle tires, you'll need a way to inflate them after you perform the repair. You can buy both hand pumps and foot

pumps, but most people will have more strength in their legs than in their hands so a foot pump might be a better option. It would probably be a good idea to purchase one that has a built-in pressure gauge so you will be able to see when you have inflated the tire to the proper PSI.

68. **Silicone and Caulk:** You never know when you'll need to seal some kind of a leak. If you shop around at your local home improvement stores, you'll find every type of sealant under the sun.

    Silicone is a good all-purpose type of sealant but you might want to have some other types on hand as well. One that comes to mind would be roofing sealant. You can even buy roofing sealant that can be applied when your roof is wet.

    Whatever type of sealant you choose to buy, make sure that you buy the right size of tube to fit in the particular caulking gun that you own.

69. **Caulking Gun:** If you need to make repairs to leaky windows or roofs, you may need a hand-

powered caulking gun. While you can purchase silicone and caulk that comes in a tube similar to the way that toothpaste is packaged, most of the time it will come in hard cardboard tubes with a plastic nozzle. Because the tube is rigid, you can't just squeeze it like a toothpaste tube. Caulking guns are really cheap, and without one you'll find it next to impossible to get the particular type of sealant you're using out of the tube without cutting a hole in the tube.

70. **Glue and Epoxy:** Keeping in mind that you'll likely have to make many repairs during an end of days scenario, it would be a good idea to have several types of glue and epoxy on hand. A few specific types you might want to consider storing are Super Glue® (cyanoacrylate), Gorilla Glue®, a variety of two-part epoxies, and J-B® Weld.

Super Glue® is actually the name used to describe cyanoacrylate adhesive, a type of glue designed to form a quick bond. While this type of glue is certainly good at sticking your fingers together instantly, many people have difficulties using it because they purchase a variety that doesn't have a really quick bond time.

You can purchase this type of glue in a variety of formulations. If you've used this type of glue in the past and had a difficult time getting it to make the bond, consider purchasing a formulation that is designed to bond the surfaces in 5 or 10 seconds. This formulation will bond the two pieces of material you are working on very quickly, but keep in mind you won't have much time to get the parts positioned properly before it sets.

Another thing worth knowing about this type of glue is that if you are gluing solid surfaces that are very clean and fit very well together, the liquid variety is probably the formulation that you want to use. On the other hand, if the surface is slightly porous or the fit isn't perfect, the thicker, "gel" formulation may be better suited for your application.

Gorilla Glue® also comes in a variety of formulations, but the one you might be most familiar with is the original formula. It is glue that actually expands as it cures and works its way into the nooks and crevices of the pieces you are trying to bond. It's a great type of glue to use when you are trying to bond irregularly shaped or porous items. One thing to keep in mind when using this particular type of glue is that a little goes a long way because when it cures it expands.

Epoxies also come in many different types of formulations. There are way too many to mention in this book. The main thing to know about epoxy is that it is comprised of two parts: the glue or "resin" and a hardener. When mixed together at the proper ratio, a chemical reaction takes place between the two parts which causes the epoxy to cure and the bond to form.

Just like cyanoacrylates, you can purchase formulations of epoxy that set up very quickly or formulations that take many hours to cure. The type you should use depends on your particular application. If you are working on something that will require a little time to get the parts positioned together properly, you probably don't want to use a fast-setting epoxy.

J-B® Weld is the brand name for a type of epoxy that is well known for making very strong bonds. It comes in two tubes that need to be mixed together at a 1:1 ratio.

While this product is an excellent type of epoxy, it's important to not let its name confuse you. It's very strong, but it is different than actually welding metal together. When you weld two pieces of metal together, the metal actually melts. The bond occurs when the welding rod or wire that also melts cools to room temperature. J-B® Weld, on the other hand, is an epoxy that stays on the surface of the material when it is cured. It has many practical applications but it's important to understand that the way it works is actually different than the way traditional welding works.

The original J-B® Weld in the red and black tubes is probably the most well-known formulation, but the company that manufactures it has introduced new products to their lineup, such as J-B® KwikWeld which comes in yellow and black tubes that is advertised to cure much faster. The tradeoff comes in the form of a difference in tensile strength and temperature resistance. The original formulation is advertised to have a higher tensile strength and greater resistance to heat.

The bottom line when it comes to making repairs with glues and epoxies is that the more varieties you have in your toolbox to choose from, the higher the likelihood you'll actually be able to form a bond that will hold up to the item's intended use.

71. **Saw For Cutting Firewood:**
If you'll be using firewood to cook food or heat your home, you may find that you'll have to resupply your stockpile at some point. Most people choose to use a chainsaw for this chore, but you have to assume that you may eventually run out of gas and oil. If this happens, you'll want to make sure you still have a way of cutting firewood.

Here's where a good quality hand saw comes in handy. Many people prefer to use what is called a "Bow Saw." This is basically a hand saw with a metal frame that has a coarse cutting blade. These blades are replaceable so make sure you keep several replacement blades on hand in the event that they become dull or you happen to break one.

Also, these saws come in a variety of lengths. Some people find that the longer blade lengths are a bit easier to use. If the blade is longer, you don't have to make as many strokes with the saw to cut through the log you are trying to cut. You'll have to decide for yourself what would be the ideal length for you.

Warning: Keep in mind that a cutting tool like a saw won't discriminate between a finger and a log. It will cut both so make sure you exercise caution and don't allow people who aren't capable of handling them safely access to them.

72. **Welder:** Having access to a welder and knowing how to properly and safely use it could be invaluable. Most welding machines will require that you have access to electricity, but there is a type of welding that does not require electricity. It's called "oxyacetylene welding."

It's beyond the scope of this book to explain how this process works. Suffice it to say that having the ability to weld broken metal pieces could be very valuable to you in an end-of-days scenario. Not to mention that if you have this ability, you may be able to trade your welding services for services or goods someone else has that you want or need.

Of course, if you plan on storing welding supplies, make sure you have a good quality welding helmet on hand, as well as high quality welding gloves and any other safety supplies that welding requires.

Warning: Due to the flammable nature of the supplies necessary for oxyacetylene welding, be sure to store and handle them safely and properly. Additionally, make sure you get the proper training for any kind of welding you

*plan on doing and that you only weld in a
safe location away from any combustible
materials.*

73. **Washable Diapers:** If you have
infants to care for in a survival situa-
tion, you may eventually run out of disposable diapers.
In this case, it would be a good idea to have a supply
of washable cloth diapers.

People have been using these types of diapers for
thousands of years. Even though most people typically
use disposable diapers these days, some people actually
still prefer to use cloth diapers. If you choose to use
them, make sure you have a way of
properly laundering them for sanita-
tion purposes.

74. **Baby Formula & Food:** If you think
you'll have infants that you'll need to
care for during a survival situation,
make sure you don't forget to stockpile baby formula
and baby food. Remember, these items also have expiration dates so make sure you don't stockpile baby
food today that you plan on using 10 years from now.

Additionally, make sure you store it under the proper conditions so that extreme temperature variations
don't cause it to prematurely spoil.

75. **Candles:** Having a supply of candles stored away is always a good idea. Candles can supply light when the electricity is out and they can even be used as effective fire starters since a candle will burn much longer than a match.

It should go without saying that if you choose to use candles, you must be extremely careful and monitor them at all times. Since you're working with an open flame, there is always the risk that the candle could start a fire or burn someone. You should also make sure you only light candles in areas with adequate ventilation.

76. **Citronella Candles:** These candles aren't designed to be used indoors. Instead, they are supposed to be lit when you are outdoors and you want to keep the mosquitoes away. Citronella is believed to repel mosquitoes so having these types of candles available could be quite handy if you find yourself trying to survive in a "camping type" environment.

Warning: Never let children light candles and never leave kids unattended around them! Special precautions should also be taken to ensure that children are always properly supervised when candles are used.

77. **Tiki Torches:** It might also be a good idea to keep some Tiki torches available for providing light outdoors, but be sure to keep them out of the reach of children. If you do decide to store Tiki torches, make

sure you also store the appropriate fuel, as well as extra wicks for them.

Since the fuel used in these types of torches is flammable, make sure you store it according to the manufacturer's recommendations.

78. **Inflatable Solar Lanterns:** These are extremely handy little items to have. You simply inflate the clear balloon-like lantern which has a small solar panel attached to the top of it. Then, leave them in the sun during the day and they'll provide you with light during the night. These solar lights are pretty inexpensive and I happen to think that they're really cool!

79. **Petroleum Jelly:** This is a common item that can be an extremely useful item to have on hand. You can use it as a lubricant, and a cotton ball soaked in petroleum jelly can be used as a makeshift fire starter. These are just a couple of the many uses for this handy item.

80. **Baby Backpack:** There are two types of backpacks specifically designed for carrying a baby. The first is the type designed to cradle your baby in front of you on your chest. The second is designed to carry your baby on your back like a traditional backpack.

The basic idea is that using one of these devices can free up your hands for doing other things. If you find yourself in a survival scenario and you have an infant to care for, being able to carry them in one of these backpacks might prove to be very useful. This way you can keep your young child with you and safely monitor them while performing various chores you might need to attend to.

Don't skimp when it comes to purchasing one of these devices. If you choose to carry your child in this type of backpack, make sure it is high quality and the appropriate size. Also, make sure that it is designed well and in good condition.

81. **Survival Caches:** A survival cache can be invaluable during a survival scenario. This is basically some kind of container you have taken the time to hide somewhere contains items you might need to survive with. You can hide them wherever you like and they can be whatever size you choose.

The good thing about a survival cache is that you can resupply yourself with items you have previously stored there. Also, if you have to bug out and leave your home, you can get supplies from your caches when you need them.

If you choose to store survival supplies in caches like this, make sure you keep a good record of exactly where you have hidden them. After all, if you can't remember where they are, they won't be much good to you.

Also, make sure that whatever material you use to make your caches out of is completely waterproof. It would be quite disappointing if you had to make your way to a survival cache only to find that the items you have stored in it were no good because they had gotten wet. You may also want to include desiccant packs to absorb any water that might find its way into them.

82. **Tape:** A good prepper will have a variety of types of tape stockpiled. Some examples of kinds you may want to store are electrical tape, medical tape, masking tape, clear packing tape, duct tape, and plumber's thread seal tape.

In a doomsday scenario, there is a very high probability that some of the items you use on a day-to-day basis will eventually wear out. Having the right type of tape on hand will mean that you might be able to make some rudimentary repairs to these items and squeeze a little bit more life out of them.

You may already have the abovementioned types of tape stored, but one type you probably don't have is called "silicone self-fusing tape." This is a very specialized type of tape that will only stick to itself. It is extremely handy and can be used for many purposes. While other types of tape will fail if you attempt to seal a broken pipe or a hose with a hole in it, this type of tape may work. It's not a replacement for a proper repair, but for emergencies or quick, in-the-field repairs, this specialized tape can be extremely useful.

83. **Suture Kit:** During times of natural disasters, you may not be able to get to a doctor. Having a suture kit on hand could come in quite handy during emergency situations.

   Warning: Keep in mind that using this particular item isn't something to be taken lightly. Performing sutures on someone should only be done as a last resort and only if you have received the proper medical training to do so. All necessary precautions should be taken to prevent infection as this can be a very risky procedure. It's never advised to give someone sutures unless you are qualified to do so.

84. **Splinting Kits:** One never knows when someone might either break a bone or injure a limb. Having materials on hand that can be used for splinting could be crucial if someone in your family or group sustains an injury.

   In a pinch, many items can be used as makeshift splints, but you can purchase kits on the Internet that are designed solely for the purpose of splinting to help immobilize an injured limb. As with all other first aid procedures, make sure you take the time to get proper training on how to splint an injury.

85. **Bee Sting Kit:** While getting stung by a bee isn't life-threatening in most cases, it can be extremely uncomfortable. Children may have an especially dif-

ficult time dealing with the pain associated with a bee sting. Having something on hand that can alleviate this pain might be a good idea.

86. **EpiPen®:** This is an epinephrine auto-injector that may be prescribed by doctors to people who are prone to experiencing severe allergic reactions to various things. Some people suffer from such severe allergic reactions that the condition can be life-threatening.

    If your doctor prescribes this particular item for you or a member of your family, make sure you discuss the proper use of it with your doctor and educate all of the members in your family or bug out camp on exactly how to use it. *Seek immediate medical attention for any form of serious allergic reaction!*

87. **Cane, Crutches, or Walking Stick:** You never know when someone might sustain an injury and need the assistance of a cane or a walking stick in order to be able to walk. Rudimentary versions of these items can be constructed in the field, but you might have a particular preference as to the way they are designed. With this in mind, it may not be a bad idea to have these items prepared ahead of time.

88. **Solar Shower:** If you've ever experienced the "joy" of taking a cold shower, you would probably really

appreciate a warm or hot shower in a survival scenario. I like the solar shower kits that are available these days. You simply fill the dark black plastic bag with water, hang it in a location where it can get direct sunlight exposure, and wait for the sun to warm it up. Then you'll have free hot water that will be a really enjoyable luxury.

89. **Portable Shower Enclosure:** If you go to the trouble of buying and setting up a solar shower kit, you probably don't want to take a shower while you're fully dressed. You can purchase shower enclosures that can be hung up or you can easily make your own by bending a piece of flexible plastic pipe into the form of a circle. Connect the ends with a plastic coupling designed to fit the particular pipe that you're using. Then attach a regular opaque shower curtain to it. With the help of some cordage, you're ready to hang it from a nearby tree. Your makeshift shower will be round, but it will provide you the privacy of being able to take a shower without your clothes on, which is always nice.

90. **Shampoo:** If you've taken the time to prepare so that you'll have the luxury of a warm shower, you'll probably want to be able to wash your hair. You might be able to save money by purchasing shampoo in bulk size containers and then transferring it to smaller con-

tainers that are easier to manage. One tip is to dilute the shampoo with water to make it last longer.

91. **Lice-Killing Shampoo:** If you have a situation arise where you have to ration your water, you may not have the luxury of being able to wash your hair on a daily basis. Many other people who haven't done as much as you have to prepare may not be able to

wash their hair at all. This could present ideal conditions for a widespread lice infestation.

Hopefully, you won't have to deal with this problem, but if you

do, you'll be glad you thought ahead and stored special shampoo formulated to kill lice.

92. **Soap:** Having access to soap will be crucial if you want to maintain good personal hygiene. Washing up *WITH SOAP* and not just rinsing off with water may help prevent the spread of germs and bacteria that could make you or people in your camp sick.

It might not be a bad idea to spend some time learning to make your own homemade soap in the event that you run out while you're still in survival mode.

93. **Soap-Making Supplies:** Soap is one of those items that you'll be using a lot of and, consequently, it might be a good idea to learn how to make your own. For thousands of years, soap was something that was

made from some very common ingredients, such as animal fat and wood ashes.

This is another one of those skills you don't want to wait to learn until you find yourself thrust into survival mode. It would be a worthwhile endeavor to learn this skill well before you actually need to use it.

Warning: Keep in mind that the wood ash will contain lye which is caustic so be sure to follow all appropriate safety precautions when working with it. Also, don't use the pot you make your soap in for cooking or any other purposes.

94. **Non-Electric Clothes Washer:** In addition to keeping your body clean, part of maintaining good personal hygiene will be keeping your clothing clean as well. If you are fortunate enough to have a generator, you'll probably want to conserve the gasoline you have stored for emergency situations, and doing laundry doesn't really qualify as an emergency. Consequently, you'll want to have some way of washing your clothing by hand.

You can either purchase commercially manufactured laundry machines that don't require electricity, or you can even use one of the many resources on the Internet to construct your own. In a pinch, you can even use an old-fashioned washboard and wash tub.

Regardless of which type you choose to use, it's probably a good idea to practice using it before you need to rely on it in an emergency situation. This would also be a good time to make sure that the particular type of laundry soap you plan on stockpiling will actually work for your needs in a grid-down scenario.

95. **Laundry Soap:** As mentioned above, you'll want to make sure that whatever type of laundry soap you choose to store will actually work in the non-electric clothes washing device that you choose to use.

    When it comes to storing laundry detergent that you will use in this type of a device, keep in mind you will probably be washing your clothing in either slightly warm or cold water. With this in mind, make sure you purchase a type of laundry detergent that will be appropriate for those conditions.

96. **Clothes Drying Line:** In a situation where the power grid is down, you obviously won't be able to dry your clothing in your electric clothes dryer. For thousands upon thousands of years, people have been drying their clothes by hanging them on a drying line and there's really no reason you can't do the same in a survival situation.

If you haven't prepared one
ahead of time, 550 paracord
can make a very good impro-
vised clothes drying line. It's
really strong so you can tension it enough to keep the line

from sagging and your clothing from dragging on the
ground. If you're like most preppers, you'll probably
have plenty of it lying around.

97. **Clothespins:** Unless you want to spend your whole
    day picking up clothing that has fallen off the line due
    to the wind blowing and re-washing them, you'll want
    to have a good supply of clothespins on hand. They're
    inexpensive and they last for a very long time so
    there's no excuse to not have plenty stored up.

98. **Deodorant:** When you're forced to spend time with
    people in cramped conditions like a tent or a bug out
    shelter, you'll really appreciate having a supply of this
    item. It will make coexisting with the people around
    you much more tolerable. Do you need deodorant to
    survive? No, but it can make the struggle of surviving
    much more tolerable.

99. **Baby Powder:** Those of you who have ever spent
    much time hiking know how unbearable it can be
    when you develop chaffing in your "nether regions."
    Having a supply of baby power may help alleviate this

discomfort. A bonus is that it's really lightweight so packing it in your bug out bag shouldn't be a problem.

100. **Sunscreen:** This is a very easy item to overlook when it comes to emergency preparedness planning. If you happen to be headed out for a weekend  at the beach, it's very natural to remember to bring sunscreen along, but when it comes to storing emergency supplies, we're not really planning for a day at the beach. Regardless, it's an essential item to have stockpiled.

Remember that a lot of the chores you may find yourself tasked with will be things like gathering firewood, collecting water, scavenging for supplies, working in your garden, hunting, and fishing. All of these activities have one thing in common and that is that you really can't do them indoors. This means you stand a high likelihood of developing sunburn if you don't have a good supply of sunscreen on hand.

Since you don't know how long you may find yourself having to survive after a natural disaster or a breakdown in civilized society, this is probably an item you would want to buy in bulk. It's probably much more cost-effective to purchase it in gallon jugs and then transfer it to smaller containers as you need to use it for the ease of portability.

101. **Tweezers:** We all know how irritating it can be when we get a sliver. While this can be a minor annoyance in the beginning, if you leave the sliver in, it could develop into an infection. I once got a tiny piece of hay stuck under my fingernail while feeding our horses, and in a matter of a few days I had developed a full blown infection in my finger that required medical care and antibiotics. Tweezers are cheap and they don't take up much space so I highly recommend having a few pairs stashed away in your first aid kit.

102. **Hemorrhoid Cream:** Believe it or not, developing hemorrhoids is a very common medical condition. If you've never experienced the discomfort they can cause, trust me when I say that you WILL want to have a supply of a good quality hemorrhoid cream stored with your emergency supplies.

103. **Nicotine Gum:** If you have a smoking habit and you suddenly find yourself without the ability to obtain cigarettes, this might be a great time to kick the habit. Having access to nicotine gum may help you through the transition period as your body adjusts to you not smoking on a daily basis. Just make sure you don't let children have access to this item. They probably won't realize that it's not just regular gum.

104. **Anti-Itch Cream:** When placed in a bug out situation and trying to survive in the wilderness,

you're probably going to be bitten by mosquitoes, biting flies, or other pesky critters. While anti-itch cream isn't generally a necessity, it may help  to alleviate the discomfort caused by the incessant itching associated with various types of bug bites. You may also appreciate this item if you happen to make contact with a particular plant that causes you a skin irritation that results in annoying itching.

105. **Antifungal Cream:** While we're on the topic of anti-itch cream, it would be a good time to bring up antifungal cream. If you've ever had a bad case of athlete's foot, you know just how uncomfortable the incessant itching can be. Not only can antifungal cream help to alleviate the irritating itching, it may also help control the fungus that is causing the problem in the first place.

106. **Bug Spray:** Speaking of mosquitoes and biting insects, having access to some form of a bug spray, such as mosquito repellent, can help prevent some of the discomfort that might come from being bitten by these types of insects.

If you have livestock, such as horses, that you intend to use for transportation or other chores during a doomsday scenario, it would be a good idea to take the time to store a supply of fly spray that is specifically designed for use on them.

107. **Mosquito Netting:** Being bitten by mosquitoes can be more than just a minor inconvenience. Mosquitoes have been known to spread diseases such as malaria. Having mosquito netting or a mosquito hood that you can wear over your head can help prevent being bitten by these nasty little critters. If you end up having to camp in a heavily mosquito-infested area, life  could be quite miserable without some way of protecting yourself from them.

108. **Eye Drops:** Eye drops can help relieve the discomfort caused by allergies or dry, itchy eyes. Again, this isn't usually a necessity, but it would be a nice comfort item.

109. **Antibacterial Liquid Hand Sanitizer:** As we all know, maintaining good personal hygiene standards can go a long way towards the prevention of spreading infectious illnesses and diseases. When you don't

have the option of washing up with soap and water, antibacterial hand sanitizer may help you to maintain cleanliness.

110. **Antacids:** You never know when you're going to come down with a case of heartburn, especially if you are suddenly forced to live on your food storage and you're not eating the types of meals you would normally eat. While the occasional case of minor heartburn isn't typically a life-threatening condition, it can be quite uncomfortable so having a supply of antacids would probably be a good idea.

111. **Feminine Hygiene Supplies:** Regardless of what Mother Nature might throw at us, a woman's body won't put things on hold. Consequently, life will become pretty unpleasant for women who don't have feminine hygiene products stockpiled. These items can be purchased in bulk quantities at various warehouse-type stores.

112. **Teeth Cleaning Supplies:** If you're like many people, your dentist probably tells you that you're not brushing and flossing enough when you go in

for a checkup. During a long-term survival situation

it's even more important to take good care of your teeth. After all, you most likely won't be able to schedule an appointment to have a cavity filled in a doomsday scenario.

With this in mind, make sure you store plenty of toothpaste, toothbrushes, floss, and mouthwash. If you take really good care of your teeth, you should be less likely to develop cavities and toothaches.

113. **Loud Signaling Horn:** If you're lost in the wilderness and you need to signal for help, having a loud signaling horn may help attract the attention of potential rescuers. My favorite type is the kind that comes with a can of compressed air so all you have to do is push a button to sound a loud blast from the horn.

If you don't have this item, you should at least keep a signaling whistle with you. If you're ever lost in the wilderness, a loud whistle could make it easier for the people who might be looking for you to actually find you.

114. **Scanner:** If you have a scanner, whether it's a handheld portable scanner or one that is installed at your home or in your vehicle, you may be able to monitor emergency frequencies so you will hopefully have some kind of an idea about what the local emergency

personnel are doing in your area. You may also be able to receive important emergency and weather broadcasts on a scanner.

Keep in mind that unless you have the necessary frequencies programmed into your scanner, it will be of little use to you. As a precaution, it would probably be a good idea to keep a printed copy of any emergency frequencies you might need to monitor. This way, if something happens and your scanner needs to be reprogrammed, you'll have access to them.

Another thing you might want to consider is installing an outdoor scanner antenna. You can even purchase external scanner antennas that are designed to be deployed in the field. These antennas may often significantly improve the reception of your emergency scanner.

115. **550 Paracord:** This is an item that has so many uses in survival that it would be impossible to list them all here. One of the main benefits and reasons that this is a particularly popular type of cordage amongst survivalists is that it has a very high strength-to-weight ratio.

If you spend a few minutes doing an online search, you can find some pretty good deals on bulk quantities of this item. Since it has so many uses in survival situations, it would probably be a good idea to have quite a bit of it on hand.

116. **Rope:** Having a good supply of various types of rope available to use would be quite beneficial as well. While 550 paracord has many uses in survival situations, it's not the solution for every need. There may be circumstances where you'll need much more robust rope, such as when you have to use a block and

tackle to lift heavy items or even if you find yourself in a situation where you need to rappel down a cliff. Having the right type of rope for the particular job at hand is very important.

117. **Carabiners and Other Climbing Equipment:** As mentioned above, there may be certain circumstances where you'll need to rappel off of a cliff to get to your destination. This isn't something you typically want to jury-rig, so having the proper carabiners and climbing equipment is essential to do this safely.

Keep in mind that the inexpensive carabiners you find in most stores are not designed to hold the weight of a person. If you are going to use climbing equipment, buy the proper kind from a mountain climbing supply store.

Warning: Never attempt to rappel down or climb up anything unless you have received the proper training to do so safely. Also, make sure that you always use the appropriate safety gear and that your equipment isn't damaged in any way.

118. **Locks:** During a survival situation there will be people who haven't prepared who are roaming the streets looking for places to steal from. Having strong padlocks available to use may help secure your important survival items from would-be thieves.

119. **Strong Metal Chains:** If you have valuable survival items that you don't want to get stolen, it's probably a pretty good idea to lock them up with heavy duty chains. If you decide to store this item, make sure it's robust enough that it won't be easily cut by looters.

There's no guarantee that locking your belongings up with heavy duty locks and chains will prevent them from being stolen. Securing them with these items, however, may dissuade thieves who aren't equipped to easily cut through the locks or chains. This is one of those situations when doing something is better than doing nothing at all.

120. **Bolt Cutters:** If you store chain so that you can lock up your precious survival items, you'll want to have a way to cut it to your desired length and bolt cutters are one tool that can be used for this task.

You can purchase short-handled bolt cutters or long-handled bolt cutters. The type with the longer handles will give you more leverage and should make the process of cutting heavy chain easier.

121. **Hand-Powered Meat Grinder:** You may have to resort to hunting or trapping to put meat on your table during a survival scenario. Having access to a hand-powered meat grinder may help ensure that you'll be able to maximize the meat you're able to harvest from a particular animal. This item may also come in handy if you happen to be raising animals that you intend to eventually butcher for food.

122. **Snares and Traps:** Having a supply of materials you can make snares out of, as well as a collection of premade traps, could help provide food for you in a doomsday scenario. You may also want to consider attaching a bell to your snares to alert you when you have actually caught something.

123. **Wildlife Bait:** If you've ever spent any time hunting, you know it can be a very time-consuming and labor-intensive task. You can often spend an entire day or even a week on a hunting expedition and come up completely empty-handed. During a survival situation, this might not be the best use of your time as there will be many other chores that need attending to.

One possible way of improving the odds of successfully bagging game to feed your family is to bait areas where game is likely to frequent. For example, if your quarry of choice is big game, such as deer, you might want to put out some grain, apples, or even salt blocks to improve your odds.

The main idea behind this strategy is that different forms of wildlife are often opportunistic in nature. If there is an abundant food source, or something that they find especially tasty at a particular location, they may be more likely to return to that location on a regular basis. This may mean you won't have to spend as much time hiking through the woods trying to find meals for your family.

It's important to understand that in many parts of the United States baiting wild game is against the law, and I certainly don't advise that you break any laws. If you decide to hunt over bait, make absolutely certain that it is legal to do so where you will be hunting.

124. **Flagging Tape:** You may not be familiar with this product, but it's very handy if you spend much time

hiking through the woods. Despite its name, flagging tape isn't really tape at all. It's actually a thin, non-adhesive plastic ribbon material that comes on a roll similar to the way tape is packaged.

Its primary purpose is to be tied to trees or branches to serve as a marker that is easily visible. Since it comes in a variety of colors and patterns, it's often quite easy to see when it's tied to a branch in the forest.

There are a number of uses for this particular item in a survival situation. For example, it can be used for marking your trail during a hunting expedition so you'll be able to find your way back to camp. It can also be used as a way of leaving indicators for other members of your group that may have gotten separated from you. This can help them determine the direction you are heading so they can catch up with you and rejoin your group.

125. **Knife-Sharpening Kit with Honing Oil:** You'll probably need to use a knife many times in a survival situation. Since you will be using your knife a lot, it will eventually become dull and need to be sharpened.

A knife-sharpening kit can help maintain a sharp cutting edge on your cutlery and survival knives. Some wet stones require the use of honing oil so make sure you store the supplies appropriate for your particular knife-sharpening kit.

Warning: Use caution and follow all necessary safety procedures when sharpening, using, or handling knives. Additionally, keep knives out of the hands of children or those who aren't able to handle them safely.

126. **Solar-Powered Electric Fence Charger:** Having the ability to set up an electric fence may be beneficial to you in more ways than one. For example, if you have animals, such as horses or cows, you'll want to make sure you have a way to keep them inside their enclosures. A solar-powered fence charger may enable you to keep your fence operable even if the power grid goes down.

Another benefit to having an electric fence is if you are growing a garden to provide food. This type of fence may help to keep wild animals, such as deer, from helping themselves to your precious vegetables.

127. **Electric Fence Supplies:** You'll also want to have the necessary supplies to actually install and maintain an electric fence. These include items like metal T-posts, insulators, electric fence wire or rope, and connectors.

128. **T-Post Pounder:** If you're going to be using T-posts to set up an electric fence, you'll want a T-post pounder. Trust me when I say that trying to drive T-posts with a sledgehammer will drive you absolutely batty.

A T-post pounder is a heavy metal tube that is capped on one end. It will have handles on either side so you can place it over a T-post, raise it up, and then let it drop or pull it down to strike the top of the T-post. This particular tool is designed to make driving T-posts much easier.

129. **Spear:** A spear can be used for self-defense, but it can pull double-duty and help you put food on the table as well. You may want to consider constructing a spear that is longer than you are tall. The reason for this is that the extra length may help ward off potential threats. As with all sharp and pointy objects, keep this item away from children.

130. **Fishing Gear:** If you happen to live near a body of water that has fish in it, you'll probably want to keep a well-stocked supply of fishing tackle on hand.

Make sure you include a variety of different types of fishing poles, as well as fishing line and the particular types of lures known to work in your area. As many fishermen already know, you can spend all day trying to catch a fish, but if you don't have the right lure or bait, you probably won't catch a thing.

131. **Lightweight Canoe:** If you plan on fishing to supply food for your family, a lightweight canoe that is easy to carry could be very useful. Make sure you also store extra paddles and that you have *and use* the appropriate safety gear, such as life jackets.

You may also want to store products that can be used to patch a canoe that gets a hole in it. For example, if your canoe is made of fiberglass, you may want to keep some fiberglass patching supplies on hand.

132. **Canoe Cart:** In a doomsday scenario, anything that isn't locked up or hidden very well will likely be stolen. Instead of leaving your canoe at the  lake or river you plan on fishing in, a canoe cart can be used to more easily transport it to and from your favorite fishing hole.

These devices are lightweight and simple in design. They basically consist of two wheels and a way of strapping your canoe to the cart. Don't let their simplistic design fool you. They are worth their weight in gold if you end up needing to transport a canoe over long distances. Even a lightweight canoe will become quite cumbersome to carry if you have to pack it very far.

133. **Salt:** Having a supply of salt on hand can be useful for not only seasoning your food, but can also be used to preserve meat and the hides of any animals you may have harvested. Additionally, it can provide a source of iodine in your diet.

134. **Electrical Wire, Connectors, and Crimping Tools:** You could find yourself having to make repairs to electrical  wires. If you do, having the proper type of connectors and/or crimping tools will improve your chances of being able to perform the job properly instead of jury-rigging it just to get the device working again. When it comes to working with electricity, this isn't the time to be jury-rigging things.

   Warning: If you're not qualified to be working on electrical devices, leave this task to someone who has the necessary skills and training to do so safely. Even if you are qualified, make absolutely certain that you always follow all applicable safety procedures.

135. **Butane Soldering Iron and Supplies:** You may find that you'll need to make repairs to electronic devices that require the use of a soldering iron. A butane-powered soldering iron doesn't need elec-

tricity which means it may be uniquely useful in a survival situation. Make sure you also store the appropriate type of solder, flux, and any other sup-plies you may need to perform the repair properly.

Warning: Be sure to follow the manufacturer's safety instructions precisely to minimize your chances of being burned while using this item. Additionally, only qualified people should perform repairs on electronic devices. If repairs are made to electronic devices improperly, it may pose a safety or fire hazard.

136. **Baling Wire:** For those of you who didn't grow up on a farm, you may not know what baling wire is. Basically, it's just a strong, flexible wire that can be used to secure any number of things. In days past, it's been used for many makeshift repairs because of its ease of use and widespread availability. It's an inexpensive item that can be purchased at most any farm supply store.

137. **Baling Twine:** As technology has advanced, hay farmers have switched from using baling wire to baling twine because of its ease of use, cheaper cost, and versatility. If you don't own livestock that eat hay, you can easily get this material simply by talking to people who do.

Every time someone cuts open a bale of hay, they're left with two or three long strands of baling twine. Over time, they end up accumulating quite a bit of this twine that they usually just end up throwing away. If you talk to someone you know who owns livestock, they'll probably be very happy if you take their old baling twine off their hands.

You can store it in a large plastic garbage bag and have access to a virtually unlimited supply of cordage that you didn't pay a single penny for. Here's a tip. Coil each strand of baling twine and tie it off with a bow. Otherwise, you'll just end up with a big bag of tangled twine.

138. **Roof Sealant and Brushes or Trowels:** For those of you who are homeowners, you know that there is always something that needs to be repaired. If your roof should happen to develop a leak, it would be a good idea to have some type of roof sealant and the appropriate brushes and/or trowels to apply it with. Having access to the proper supplies to repair a leaky roof will not only keep you dry, it can also prevent costly damage to the interior of your home.

139. **Plastic Sheeting:** I highly suggest you store a large quantity of plastic sheeting. There are many uses for this item. You can do everything from repairing a bro-

ken window to sealing your windows and doors in the event that the air in your particular area becomes contaminated. You can use it to construct makeshift emergency shelters and clear plastic can even be used to make a solar still for collecting water.

Something that's worth knowing when it comes to purchasing plastic sheeting is that it is sold in different thicknesses. The term "mil" is used to describe the thickness of sheets of plastic. One mil is equivalent to one thousandth of an inch or 0.001". So a 5 mil plastic sheet will be 0.005" thick. The higher the mil number, the thicker the plastic. When you purchase plastic sheeting, it will be more likely to tear or puncture easily. if it has a very low mil rating.

Warning: Large plastic sheets can pose a suffocation hazard. Keep this item out of the hands of children and people who aren't mentally or physically capable of handling it safely.

140. **Plastic Tarps:** The uses that plastic tarps have in survival situations are virtually limitless. They can be used for everything from creating a makeshift tent to keeping yourself off the cold, wet ground while sleeping.

These are inexpensive items that don't take up much storage space so I highly suggest you purchase a wide variety of plastic tarps in many shapes and sizes. Like plastic sheeting, tarps come in various thicknesses. Keep this in mind when you are purchasing them.

141. **Extra Blankets:** If you find yourself without electricity and don't have a safe alternative method of heating your home, a good supply of extra  blankets may help keep your family warm during the long, cold winter nights. This isn't just a matter of comfort either. Having the ability to keep warm could mean the difference between life and death in a survival situation.

142. **Extra Shoes or Boots:** Depending on how long you have to survive, you may wear out your old shoes or boots. Therefore, it's a good idea to store a few extra pairs, just in case.

 If you have children who are still growing, you'll want to make sure you have an assortment of various types of footwear on hand in larger sizes so they'll have something to wear as they grow.

Some good sources of inexpensive footwear are thrift stores and yard or garage sales. You may not be able to purchase the latest fashions, but you'll find a virtually endless supply of very inexpensive shoes and boots at places like these.

143. **Shoe GOO®:** This is a particular type of glue specifically designed for repairing shoes and boots. I've used it on many occasions and it can be quite effective. In my opinion, this is a must-have item for any prepper. As a bonus, it can be used for many other purposes than simply repairing footwear.

144. **Spare Shoelaces:** For those of you who have spent a day walking around with one broken shoelace, you know why it's important to store this item. Now, I should point out that I actually advise you replace the laces in your shoes and boots with 550 paracord since it is much stronger than regular laces.

Regardless of whether or not you choose to take this advice, the important thing is that you have something on hand to replace your laces when they do break. In a survival situation, good footwear will be vital. Broken laces will slow you down significantly if you don't have the means of replacing them.

145. **Weather Forecasting Equipment:** Having equipment you can use to help predict the weather can be quite beneficial. After all, you'll still want to be able to plan your outdoor activities around the upcoming

weather conditions. For example, if you have some method of predicting an oncoming winter storm, you'll be better prepared to make critical decisions that could affect your ability to survive.

You can purchase battery-powered devices designed for this purpose, but it might also be a good idea to have some battery-free equipment on hand, such as a non-electric barometer, an old-fashioned thermometer, and maybe even a wind gauge.

146. **Spray Paint:** Keeping a can of red or orange spray paint with you can make it possible to leave important messages for people. For example, if your family happens to be sick with a pandemic illness, you could spray-paint a notice on your door letting others know that your house is under quarantine so they don't come into your home and become infected as well.

    This item can also be used to leave messages for

people in your bug out group if you have to leave without them. You can leave cryptic messages that will alert them to the location you are headed so they can meet you there.

147. **Binoculars:** This item can be used to help when you are hunting for food, but it can also be used

to perform long-range surveil-
lance on looters and marauders
that might be approaching your
property or bug out camp.

This is an item that is worth
spending a little extra money on. Low quality binoculars don't allow much light to pass through the lens
which can make using them difficult in low light conditions such as dawn or dusk.

Some even have the ability to adjust the level of
magnification on them. This can be a very handy fea-
ture because you may need to use them to view wildlife or people at various distances.

148. **Spare Eyeglasses and/or Contact Lenses:** If you
have poor vision and need to
wear eyeglasses or contacts to
see properly, it might be a good
idea to keep an extra set on hand.

In the case of contact lenses, you should probably
keep a supply of several extra pairs. You should also
keep a generous amount of eyeglass and/or contact
cleaning supplies stored up.

Even if your vision is fine, you might want to have
some sunglasses and/or safety glasses available to use.
Keep this in mind. If you sustain an injury to your eyes
because you weren't wearing safety glasses, the task of
surviving will become much more difficult.

149. **Eyeglass Repair Kit:** Those of you who wear glasses already know it can be quite an inconvenience if a lens pops out or some other part of your glasses need to be repaired and you don't have an eyeglass repair kit available to use. These kits are very inexpensive and can be purchased at virtually any store. They come with a small screwdriver, a variety of small screws that are commonly used in eyeglasses, and a variety of different nose pads.

If you wear glasses, this is another must-have item to keep on hand. In a survival situation, if your glasses break and you don't have the ability to repair them, it's going to make surviving the challenges you are faced with that much more miserable.

150. **Maps of Your Area:** Having maps of your area could come in very handy as well. They can help you find alternative escape routes if you have to leave the city  and one particular road happens to be congested because everyone else is trying to evacuate at the same time. They can also help you by letting you know where the nearest body of water is if you have to scavenge for water when your supplies run out.

151. **Compass:** If you're going to store a map, you should also have a compass. That being said, a compass will be of little use to you if you don't know how to  use it properly. I suggest you not only purchase a good quality compass, but that you take the time to learn how to use it to navigate in conjunction with your map.

In the day and age that we live in, where most people have access to a GPS, the art of orienteering is all but lost. Fortunately, there are many books you can purchase, as well as multiple online resources to teach you how.

Orienteering is a skill that needs to be practiced to become proficient at it. The time to practice is now rather than later when you suddenly find yourself struggling to live through a survival situation.

152. **GPS:** While maps are valuable because they allow you to see an entire geographical region at one glance, a GPS may be easier for people to navigate with. Most people are more familiar with GPS navigation than they are with using paper maps and a compass, so you probably should store a quality GPS with a supply of extra batteries.

Make sure you keep the instruction manual handy in case you need to reference it during an emergency.

The time to learn how to use your GPS is not when you end up in a survival situation. Spend the time now learning how to use it so that when you need to rely on it, you'll already have the necessary skills.

The GPS I use when we go horseback riding, geocaching, or hiking, has a small but robust antenna that helps the device maintain a constant signal with the satellite network. I like to wear my GPS around my neck for easy access when I'm riding or hiking. My old one would constantly lose the signal if it flipped over so that the screen was touching my chest. Because my new GPS has this small antenna, I don't lose the signal unless I'm in a very densely forested area.

153. **Canteens:** If the need arises and you have to head out on an expedition to search for additional resources, you'll want to have a way of conveniently carrying water with you. Canteens come in a number of shapes and sizes to accommodate virtually every possible scenario.

   One very popular style is designed to be worn like a backpack. This version usually has a flexible rubber hose that you can use like a drinking straw when you need to rehydrate. I like this kind, but it does have a drawback, in my opinion. If you're wearing it on your back like a backpack, it can be difficult to wear an actual backpack you might need to carry other supplies in. I guess you could put this type of canteen inside your backpack, but this would slightly reduce the amount of gear you could carry in your pack.

Only you can decide what type of canteen you would like to carry, but my personal preference is a stainless steel metal canteen that can be carried in a pouch on a belt. I prefer a metal canteen for a couple of reasons. The first is that I just feel like they are more robust and less likely to develop a leak than one made out of cheap plastic.

The other reason, and the main reason I prefer a metal canteen, is that I could use it as a vessel to boil water in if I were to end up in a situation where I have to scavenge for water and collect it from a river or stream. Regardless of which style you choose to carry, the point is that  you should always have a way of carrying water with you.

154. **Holsters and Slings:** Many preppers choose to incorporate firearms into their emergency preparedness planning. One thing that shouldn't be overlooked is that, in a prolonged doomsday type scenario, you may find yourself having to hike over

long distances. While you are hiking, it can be very helpful if you have a convenient way of carrying your weapon of choice. If it's a handgun, you'll probably want a good quality holster. If you'll be carrying a rifle, you may want a good quality sling or scabbard.

This will allow you to carry your weapon with you while keeping your hands free to do other chores and tasks. Depending on the weight of your particular firearm, the right holster or sling may also make the job of carrying it much less physically demanding.

While you are thinking about how you will carry your particular firearm, it would be a good idea to think about how you'll carry additional ammunition as well. If you'll be carrying a revolver, this will present some unique challenges for keeping extra ammunition accessible, but if you are carrying a semi-automatic handgun or rifle, there are many accessories you can purchase to make it easy to keep extra magazines on your body and conveniently available.

155. **Firearm Cleaning Supplies:** Gun enthusiasts understand the importance of keeping their firearms clean and properly oiled. If you're

not an avid shooter or you're new to the world of firearms, you really should adopt this philosophy. A firearm that is kept clean and properly lubricated will usually be more likely to function properly when you need to use it.

Warning: If you choose to incorporate firearms into your emergency preparedness planning, make sure you take special precautions to keep both the firearms and ammunition secure and out of the hands of children or those who aren't capable of using or handling them safely. Also make sure you have been properly trained in firearm safety and that you always follow any and all appropriate safety practices.

156. **Bladed Weapons:** I'm a big fan of bladed weapons because they can be used repeatedly without the need to reload or carry extra ammunition. Some  examples of bladed weapons you might consider storing are knives, machetes, survival axes and hatchets, and/or spears.

Warning: Keep in mind that bladed weapons can pose significant safety hazards so make sure you keep them out of the hands of anyone who isn't able to safely handle them.

157. **Primitive Weapons:** Having a collection of primitive weapons, such as a bow and arrow, a slingshot, or an atlatl, could be very valuable to you. They can be used for self-defense as well as for hunting.

Be aware that they'll be of little use to you if you haven't taken the time to become proficient with them. The time to practice is now rather than when your belly is rumbling because you haven't eaten in a few days.

At the risk of sounding redundant, remember that although primitive, these are still potentially dangerous weapons. With this in mind, make sure that people who aren't capable of handling them safely don't have access to them.

158. **Pepper Spray:** Pepper spray is often chosen for non-lethal self-defense. It comes in canisters of various shapes, sizes, and formulations. It's beyond the scope of this book to advise you on exactly what type you may want to purchase, but it might be a good idea to keep a canister of it with you in the event you find yourself having to fend off someone who may intend to do you harm.

Self-defense is a very important matter and you'll have to make the decision for yourself about how you plan on protecting yourself and your family members. It's worth pointing out that this type of self-defense product does have some limitations. For example, if the wind happens to be blowing in your direction when you use it, it may be possible to get some of it in your own eyes. This could significantly impede your vision and, consequently, your ability to defend yourself. Another limitation is that in a moment of panic, you might miss your target.

Only you can decide whether or not you want to add this to your arsenal of self-defense tools. If you do decide to utilize it, make sure you and any of your family members who plan on carrying it thoroughly understand the proper way to use it.

159. **Bear Spray:** Much like pepper spray, bear spray can be used to protect you as well. While pepper spray is intended to be used on humans, bear spray is intended to discourage a bear from attacking you. It comes in much larger canisters than the typical self-defense pepper spray you might be accustomed to.

   While there's no guarantee that it will be 100% effective, many people who spend time in the wilderness carry it as an added element of protection in the event that they come across a bear that appears to be threatening them. Keep in mind that if you choose to carry this item, you really should get proper training on how and when to use it. For example, I wouldn't personally use it if I just happened to see a bear that wasn't threatening me.

160. **Pressure Cooker:** Having access to a high quality pressure cooker may be useful to you in a survival situation because it can reduce the amount of fuel you'll have to burn in order to cook your food. Pressure cookers are designed to cook food more quickly than traditional pots and pans which may be very beneficial to you, especially if you have a limited supply of fuel to use for cooking.

One thing to keep in mind when it comes to pressure cookers is that they are not all created equal. This certainly isn't the type of item you want to buy at a bargain store. If you happen to have your grandmother's pressure cooker stashed away in your cupboard, it's probably time to upgrade to a newer version that is equipped with modern safety features.

Also keep in mind that due to the way these pots work, low quality or outdated varieties could be quite dangerous to use. High quality, modern pressure cookers should have safety features that are designed to release the pressure in the event it becomes too high. These safety features are intended to help prevent the risk of explosion, which is why I don't recommend purchasing one that isn't very well designed and equipped with functioning safety features.

If you decide to utilize this particular type of pot in your emergency preparedness cooking plans, make sure you thoroughly familiarize yourself with how to use it safely and that you follow all of the manufacturer's instructions in order to prevent being burned or injured while using it.

161. **Dutch Ovens:** If you've never used a Dutch oven before, you probably don't have any idea how useful they can be

in an off-the-grid cooking situation. A Dutch oven is basically a heavy duty, cast iron cooking vessel. Unlike a traditional cast iron skillet you might be familiar with, a Dutch oven is equipped with a heavy duty lid, as well as a handle like you might find on a five-gallon bucket.

These versatile cooking pots can be used in traditional ovens, but their real value in a survival situation is that they can be used in a campfire quite effectively. You can cook everything from rabbit stew to bread in one. If you plan on cooking over a campfire, this really is a must-have item, in my opinion.

162. **Solar Oven:** Many people who live off the grid use solar ovens to warm their food. While you can make your own solar oven, a lot of people have learned that solar ovens are typically best suited for *warming* foods. Unless you have a very high quality model that

is designed quite well, they're not particularly good at cooking raw food that needs to be cooked at a particular temperature to make it safe to eat.

That's not to say that they don't have their place in a survival situation, but if you're cooking foods such as chicken that have to be cooked well enough to prevent salmonella poisoning, I would recommend using another source that will actually be able to raise the food to the optimal safe cooking temperature.

163. **Non-electric Food Dehydrator:** Dehydrating food is an excellent way of preserving and increasing its shelf life. If you have a food dehydrator that doesn't require electricity, you'll have a way of preserving fruits and vegetables from your garden, as well as wild edible plants and berries you might find while foraging.

    You can either purchase or make your own dehydrator that doesn't require electricity. Some rely on reflectors and solar concentrators to take advantage of the heat that the sun can provide, while others simply have some trays and an enclosure made of a mesh-like material to keep insects away from the food you're dehydrating.

164. **Wood Fired Smoker:** Smoking is an age-old technique for preserving meat. At one point in history, it was one of the primary methods for the preservation of meat. In this day and age, some people have

smokers but they are very small and often require electricity.

When preparing for a doomsday scenario that lasts for a prolonged period of time, it might be better to build an outdoor wood-fired smokehouse that can be used for smoking something like an entire deer at once.

An important note about using a wood smoker is that the time to learn how to use it is not during a major crisis. If you live in an area where you will have the ability to hunt for food, take the time now to learn how to properly preserve meat by smoking it. Then, if the day should ever come when you have to rely on this knowledge, you'll be better prepared.

165. **Rocket Stove:** This is a specially designed cooking stove that burns small pieces of wood, such as twigs and branches. The way it is designed makes it very efficient at using small twigs and branches to achieve temperatures suitable for cooking.

Because of the way this type of stove is designed, a fire that is hot enough to cook on can be made quite quickly. Unlike cooking over a wood fire, that often requires quite a bit of time for a bed of coals to develop that will provide enough heat to cook on, a rocket stove can be fired up quite quickly for convenient wood-fired cooking.

There are many instructions on the Internet that describe how to build your own rocket stove or you can purchase one of the many commercially manufactured versions if you prefer.

Warning: Because these stoves can develop quite high temperatures, you need to be especially careful not to burn yourself when using one.

166. **Hand-Powered Juice Press:** It's no secret that juicing is an excellent way of utilizing the nutrition contained in fruits and vegetables. If you find  yourself having to survive without electricity, having access to a hand-powered juice press could be quite valuable.

   In addition to making tasty beverages, you can use it to extract juice from the parts of fruits and vegetables you would normally throw away because they might not be your favorite parts to eat.

167. **Variety of Kitchen Utensils:** I recommend everyone have hand-powered blenders, whisks, and a variety of other kitchen utensils you'll need to prepare meals with your family during a doomsday scenario.

168. **Solar Water Heater:** Solar water heaters are commonly used by people who live off the grid because they don't require natural gas, propane, or electricity

to heat the water. All they require is the power of the sun.

Keep in mind that not all solar water heaters are created equal so make sure you purchase a high quality model capable of heating your water to a high enough temperature to prevent the growth of bacteria.

Warning: Water stored in a hot water heater tank that isn't kept at a high enough temperature may grow bacteria that could cause you to catch Legionnaires' disease.

169. **Bathtub Water Bladders:** These handy devices are basically like big water balloons that can be placed in a bathtub and filled with water. Many preppers already know that you can store water in a bathtub during emergency situations, but these water bladders provide a more sanitary environment for storing water in a bathtub.

    They only cost about $25 and some models are capable of storing up to a hundred gallons of water. Many models even come with a hand pump you can use to siphon the water out of the bladder when you need to draw from it.

170. **Ice Chests:** If you have the ability to make ice or collect ice from a nearby lake or stream, you'll probably want to have a few ice chests on hand. They can increase the amount of time it takes the ice to melt. If you actually have ice and a well-insulated ice chest, they can be helpful if you're trying to keep food cool.

If you do collect ice from a lake or stream, don't ingest it because it may contain harmful microorganisms or other contaminants. Additionally, don't allow ice you have collected to make direct contact with your food or drink. Keep food and drink in sealed bags or containers to help prevent the possibility of ice contaminating anything you plan to eat or drink with germs or bacteria.

171. **Large Pot:** During the cold winter months, you may lose your ability to collect water from a nearby stream or lake. If you have a large pot that you can melt snow in, you'll be better equipped to stay hydrated and attend to your personal hygiene needs.

If you do melt snow you intend to drink, make sure you follow the recommendations from FEMA about how they advise treating water. It may appear clean because it's white and fluffy, but it could still contain harmful contaminants. I can't overstate the importance of properly filtering and treating water to hopefully avoid becoming sick. Here's the URL to the document from FEMA that I referred to earlier: www.fema.gov/pdf/library/f&web.pdf.

172. **Modern Fire-Starting Tools:** You may very well have the knowledge and skills to make a fire with a bow drill, but would you really want to if you have better tools at your disposal? Common items such as matches and butane lighters are much more convenient when it comes to starting a fire.

Also keep in mind that if you find yourself having to bug out and survive in cold temperatures, the speed at which you are able to start a fire could save your life! If the temperature is cold enough, or especially if you are wet, it doesn't take long for hypothermia to set in. Wouldn't you rather have some waterproof matches or a good quality lighter to use for starting a fire under these conditions?

That's not to say you shouldn't learn primitive fire-starting techniques you can employ during emergencies. Having these skills could also save your life, but the convenience of modern fire-starting tools should make it much easier to start a fire. This is true for situations when your life depends on it, as well as those times when you just want to warm up a can of beans.

173. **Campfire Rotisserie Device:** A metal rack you can put food on and slowly rotate over a campfire can be very useful if you actually end up having to cook over a fire. These items can be purchased at many camping

supply stores or, if you're handy with metal fabrication, you can even make your own.

174. **Bellows:** This is a handy item that many people probably aren't even aware of. A bellows is a device that is used to blow air into a fire to rekindle it or help to get it started. Instead of spending your time on your hands and knees blowing into your campfire, you can use a bellows to direct oxygen precisely where you need it.

In case you aren't familiar with this particular item, it's basically two pieces of wood with handles on each piece. The two pieces are connected to each other with a hinge and some kind of airtight material. When you open and close the bellows, air is forced out through a small nozzle at the end. This is much more convenient and effective than trying to blow into a hot fire and running the risk of choking on the smoke or being burned.

175. **Aluminum Foil:** There are so many uses for this item in a survival situation that it would be difficult to mention them all in this book. One of my favorite uses for this particular item would be the ability to cook "hobo dinners" in a campfire.

If you're not an avid camper, you may not know what a hobo dinner is. Basically, it's the camping equivalent of an old-fashioned TV dinner. You simply put meat, vegetables, and seasonings into a foil pouch. Then you place the package into the fire coals and slowly let it cook. As the different ingredients cook, their flavors blend together and the end result is a very tasty campfire meal!

176. **Plastic Cling Wrap:** If you find yourself in a situation where you have to survive on your food storage, you'll want to make sure you don't let anything go to waste. A supply of plastic cling wrap can be used to cover your bowls so you can eat the leftovers from the food you prepared earlier at a later time. With that being said, *make sure you don't eat food that hasn't been stored at the correct temperature to keep it safe for consumption.* Also, remember that even leftovers that have been properly covered will eventually spoil. Make sure you use common sense and that you don't eat spoiled food.

    Another use for this item is simply keeping insects out of any containers that might have food temporarily stored in them. For example, if you don't eat all of your lunch and you plan on eating the leftovers for dinner that night, you can cover your plate or bowl with cling wrap to keep those pesky critters off your food.

177. **Zip Top Baggies:** I love zip top baggies and think that they're one of the greatest inventions ever made. I prefer the modern type that has the little plastic handles that you slide across the top of the baggie to

ensure that the seal is actually made. The other kind that you simply squeeze the top edge to seal the bag is more difficult for me to use. I find it can be a little bit tricky to get them complete-

ly sealed at times. It can also be kind of hard to tell if the baggie is actually completely sealed.

178. **Winter Clothing:** Since we never know exactly what the weather conditions might be if we're suddenly forced into a survival situation, I highly advise that everyone store winter clothing.

Even if you don't live in an area that typically gets cold, storing good quality winter clothing is important. For example, if you end up having to bug out and retreat to the mountains to survive in an area that's less populated, you may find yourself having to endure much colder temperatures than you're accustomed to.

179. **Hand Warmers:** There are different types of hand warmers available to purchase, but my favorite are the kind that come in a plastic package that is automatically activated when you open the package and expose it to oxygen. This prepackaged variety is a little bit easier to transport and use than the other

types. They can also be stuffed into the toes of your boots or into your gloves.

180. **Snowshoes:** If you've ever spent any amount of time trying to hike through deep snow, you know why I recommend storing this particular item. Trudging through deep snow can be back-breaking work, but if you own a good quality  pair of snowshoes and the conditions are right, you'll be able to walk on top of the snow, making traveling MUCH EASIER!

181. **Snow Sleds:** I'm not talking about the small, round, flimsy plastic saucer-type sleds that your children slide down the hill on during the winter for fun. I'm talking about utilitarian-based cargo sleds you can use to haul supplies in during the winter. I would advise against purchasing inexpensive plastic sleds that are marketed to children for wintertime fun. Instead, look for cargo sleds specifically designed to be robust enough for the job you need them to do.

There are cargo sleds designed to be pulled behind a snowmobile that are made of very tough plastic material that you might want to consider purchasing. If you've ever spent much time hiking in the snow, you know that walking can be extremely tasking. If you add elements to the mix, like carrying firewood or perhaps even transporting an injured person, having a good quality cargo sled will be invaluable.

182. **Kitty Litter:** Even if you don't own cats, you'll probably want to keep a supply of kitty litter in your vehicle. Those of us who live in areas that get plenty of snow already know that pouring some kitty litter in front of or behind your drive wheels, if you happen to get stuck, can sometimes help you gain traction and get your vehicle moving again.

183. **Extra Clothing:** You never know when your clothing might become damaged beyond repair so it's a good idea to have plenty on hand. If you have young children, it might also be a good idea to purchase some clothing at a thrift store in larger sizes in the event you have to survive for long periods of time and they outgrow their clothing that currently fits them.

184. **Cargo Pants:** I'm not talking about fashion here, but I do recommend you purchase some cargo pants. The reason I recommend these types of pants is that they have many pockets that can be useful if you have to bug out and carry a lot of items with you.

185. **Camouflage:** During a survival situation, there may be times when you want to do all that you can to remain undetected. Having camouflage clothing that is *appropriate for the environment in which you will be surviving* could be very beneficial to you.

   The main thing to keep in mind about choosing camo is that the pattern should match the environment that you'll need to conceal yourself in. For example, if you'll be bugging out in a forest full of oak trees, you probably won't want to purchase clothing in a military style desert camouflage pattern.

186. **Rain Gear:** Not only is it a good idea to store winter clothing, it's also a good idea to have some rain gear available to wear. You can purchase inexpensive emergency ponchos at most camping stores, but you might want to have some more robust and durable rain gear available to use as well.

   The emergency ponchos that are commonly available are usually simply a plastic bag with a hole cut out of the top and maybe a hood. They are constructed of very thin plastic that is easily torn so if you have to do any type of work, such as gathering or splitting firewood when it's raining, you'll want rain gear that is able to stand up to the rigors of the task.

187. **Survival Hammock:** Unlike a traditional hammock that you might have hanging in your backyard, a survival hammock is made of lightweight material that

doesn't take up much space in a backpack. Survival hammocks can make excellent emergency shelters because they can be deployed very quickly without much effort at all. They also provide a way of keeping you off the ground while you sleep and many have valuable extra features, such as mosquito netting and/or protective rain covers.

188. **Bivy Sack:** A bivy sack is similar to a survival hammock with the draw-back that it doesn't get you off of the ground. It's basically a one-person  makeshift tent that can be quickly deployed to provide added protection from the elements in a survival situation. In addition to providing some extra warmth, a bivy sack can provide a way of keeping you dry if it happens to rain during the night. Another advantage of this type of emergency shelter is that it doesn't take up as much space in a backpack as a traditional tent does.

189. **Gloves:** It would probably be a good idea to store a variety of different types of gloves, including winter, work, and rubber gloves.

190. **Plywood:** If you live in an area of the world that is prone to severe weather conditions, such as hurricanes

and tornadoes, you understand the importance of having plywood on hand. For those of us who don't live in these types of areas, it's still a good idea to have plywood available so we can board up our windows if we ever have to "bug in." Having the ability to put plywood over your windows can also help prevent vandalism from looters and marauders who might be passing by.

191. **Nails:** If you're going to store plywood, you also need to make sure you have a way of attaching the plywood to your windows. Buy several boxes of heavy-duty nails and keep them in an area where you'll be able to find them if you suddenly need to use them to prepare for an impending storm.

192. **Hammer:** Having a supply of nails won't do you much good if you don't have a way of driving them into the wood so make sure you have at least one high quality hammer on hand. I suggest you purchase one with a metal or impact-resistant fiberglass handle that is less likely to break than the kind that has a wooden handle.

193. **Bartering Items:** Think about the types of items that many people can't live without for a single day. I'm certainly not advocating you store anything illegal, but there are plenty of habits that people have and they'll

quickly run out of the necessary supplies to feed these habits.

Some examples of bartering items you might consider storing are alcohol, cigarettes, chewing tobacco, ammunition, and medical supplies. When it comes to the concept of storing bartering items, consider this. Some people might trade virtually anything they have for something like a supply of good coffee. If you happen to have these types of items on hand, you can use them as bartering chips even if you don't use them yourself.

Bartering was once a primary method of doing business but it has since become a bit of a lost art. In addition to storing bartering items, it would be well worth your time to actually practice the art of trading. If you aren't skilled, it's very easy to come out on the losing end of a trade. On the other hand, if you have honed your negotiation skills, you'll be in a much better position to make a trade that is mutually beneficial to both parties. You may even come out ahead of the game if you are really good at bartering! In a world where supplies have more value than money, this can really work to your benefit if you take the time to learn to become a skilled trader.

194. **Medical Condition Card:** It would probably be a good idea for each member in your group to carry a laminated card that lists any and all medical conditions that the particular person might have, as well as

any medications that they require. Sure, *you'll probably know* what medical conditions your family members have, but what if you happen to get separated?

If something should happen to a member of your group who gets separated from you and they experience a medical emergency, having a list of their existing medical conditions somewhere on their person could help people who may intend to render first aid know how to treat them properly.

A good example is if someone in your group happens to be a diabetic and their blood sugar drops to a critically low level. If the medical card they are carrying contains instructions about how to treat this condition, someone who happens upon them may be able to provide them with the type of care they need.

195. **Over-The-Counter Medications:** Many people think to store common over-the-counter medications such as aspirin and ibuprofen, but other types to consider would be medications like anti-diarrhea, anti-nausea, cold and flu, and antacids.

If you decide to store these types of items, keep in mind that they do have a shelf life so you don't want to stick them away in a box and find out 10 years from now that they're no good. Also, the conditions in which they are stored can significantly reduce their shelf life. If you store them in a sweltering hot garage, you may find that they won't last nearly as long as if they were stored according to the manufacturer's recommendations.

196. **Prescription Medications:** If you have health conditions that require you to take prescription medications, you may want to consider storing as much as you possibly can. As mentioned above, make sure that you don't store it past its expiration date and that you always store it in the proper conditions. For example, some medications might need to be kept refrigerated or cool to prevent them from going bad.

    Warning: Always store any medications in a location that children or people who shouldn't have access to them can't get hold of them.

197. **Diabetic Supplies:** If anyone in your group happens to be a diabetic, you should probably plan on storing extra diabetic supplies. If at all possible, tell your doctor about your emergency preparedness plans and ask if there is any medication he or she might be able to prescribe for you that doesn't require refrigeration. This could be quite beneficial during a survival situation when you might not have access to a refrigerator or ice that can be used to keep your medication cold.

198. **Contraceptives and Birth Control:** This is an item that's very easy to overlook when it comes to prepping, but it's also an item that is extremely impor-

tant to have. Remember, just because you might find yourself having to survive during a crisis, your natural human urges won't go away. This is especially true if you end up in a prolonged survival situation.

This is also an item that can be used for bartering because a lot of people won't think ahead and consequently they won't have this item on hand. If you do decide to store this item, make sure you store according to the manufacturer's recommended directions. After all, if you store it in your garage and the temperature gets to 120 degrees, it might not be of much use to you once you eventually need it.

199. **Handheld Tree Pruners:** In addition to caring for your fruit trees so they will be able to yield the most

abundant harvest possible, this device can be used to easily cut small dead branches off the lower parts of trees to be used for starting a fire.

I suggest you purchase pruners that have long handles. Having the additional length of the handles will provide you with more leverage. This extra leverage should make the chore of cutting through thicker limbs easier.

200. **Wagon:** A simple child's wagon can be used for transporting supplies such as firewood and/or water to

your camp, but I recommend you purchase a heavy duty wagon you can pick up at most farm supply or home improvement stores. These wagons are much more robust, they have pneumatic wheels which should make pulling them easier, and they can carry a much heavier load.

201. **Water Filter:** FEMA recommends that if you have to scavenge for water when your supplies run out, you always filter it. That doesn't mean it shouldn't be treated afterwards, but properly pre-filtering is always a good idea to remove any particulates that might be suspended in the water. Keep in mind that in most cases, filtering water alone doesn't necessarily make it safe to drink, but it is an essential step in the process of treating water.

202. **Money:** If you find yourself having to survive and you run out of a particular item that you need, you may be able to purchase it from someone you come in contact with. Keep in mind that if you only have a $100 bill on you, and all you need to buy are some bandages, you're going to have to pay $100 for those bandages because the person who might be willing to sell them to you probably won't have the cash on them to give you change. For this reason, I always recommend keeping small bills on hand.

203. **Books to Identify Edible Plants and Berries:** If you have to survive in a wilderness situation, you may find the need to forage for edible wild plants and berries. Having a good field guide with very clear color photos and descriptions of the individual plants that you can safely eat would be very important.

Warning: When it comes to foraging for food in the wilderness, you can't afford to take risks. Make sure that whatever you choose to eat, you're 100% sure that it's safe to do so.

204. **Spare Light Bulbs:** If you're fortunate enough to actually have electricity in the situation you find yourself having to survive in, it would be a real bummer if you didn't have light in your house simply because you didn't store extra light bulbs. While you're buying these items, make sure to buy some spare bulbs for your flashlights if they are replaceable as well.

205. **Liquid Fuel Lanterns:** liquid-fueled camping lanterns can provide quite a bit of light in a survival situation. The way these lanterns work  is you fill the reservoir with the exact type of liquid fuel that is designed for the particular lamp you are using. Then you use the built-in pump to pressurize the fuel reservoir. Lastly, you light the mantles using the manufacturer's recommended procedures.

206. **Lantern Fuel:** If you're going to plan on using liquid fuel lanterns, be sure to store the appropriate type of fuel recommended by the manufacturer of your particular lantern.

    It's worth pointing out that some modern camping lanterns are capable of using propane. Whatever type you choose to use, make sure that you store the appropriate type of fuel. Also make sure that you store the fuel according to the manufacturer's storage recommendations.

207. **Spare Mantles:** In addition to storing fuel for your lantern, you should store plenty of spare mantles. A mantle works in a similar manner that an old-fashioned wick in an oil lamp works. They are the actual part of the lantern that produces light when the lamp is lit. They kind of look like little baby stockings that are made out of a thin mesh-like material. Without them, you won't be able to light your lantern and it will be of little use

to you. Mantles won't work if they get a hole in them so be sure to handle them with care. They tend to be a little delicate at times.

208. **Rechargeable Flashlights:** If you end up having to survive in a grid-down environment, having access to flashlights during the night can make life much easier for you. Not only can they provide you with the necessary light to do your nighttime chores, they can help young children cope with this situation. A flashlight can serve as a handheld night-light and children might be less afraid if they have a comforting source of light.

Rechargeable flashlights are especially useful because when the batteries wear down, you can simply recharge them. That is, of course, if you have some kind of power source. Some models you can buy come with a hand crank you can use to charge the battery. If at all possible, you should have some of these types of flashlights on hand because they can be quickly charged even without a power source. The charge doesn't last very long, but it also doesn't take very long to crank the handle and charge them up enough to use them again.

209. **Rechargeable Headlamps:** A headlamp is probably even more useful than a flashlight because it frees your hands up to tackle any of the nighttime chores you might be faced with. The beauty of a headlamp

 is that anyplace you look, you'll have light.

You can purchase headlamps in a variety of shapes and sizes, but it might be a good idea to purchase a type that you can recharge so you don't have to store a lot of batteries for them. It should go without saying that if you are using any rechargeable devices, you'll need some way of recharging them. Make sure you don't overlook this detail when purchasing rechargeable electronic devices.

210. **Glow Sticks:** This is an item that nearly everyone is familiar with. While it's true that they don't provide much light, they can still be useful in a survival situation. Other sources of light, such as flashlights or headlamps, will provide much more light. That being said, in a true emergency where you don't have access to these other devices, a glow stick can provide a short-term source of light to help you perform basic chores during the night. They can also be used as luminescent markers during the night to help members of your bug out party identify specific locations in your camp.

211. **Cell Phone Charging Case:** While there's a very good possibility that during a major natural disaster or a doomsday scenario we won't have the ability to

use our cell phones for communications, it's still probably a good idea to prepare as if we will, just in case.

Virtually everyone has a case on their smartphone to protect it, but you may want to consider purchasing a specially designed case that is capable of actually charging your cell phone in an emergency. These cases can be very useful for preppers. They function as a regular protective case for your smartphone, but they have a built-in battery that can be used to charge your phone when its battery is dead.

In some instances, having your phone in one of these cases can double the time you'll be able to use your phone before recharging. You will eventually have to recharge both the case and the phone, but the nice thing about this accessory is that it significantly prolongs the amount of time you'll be able to use your smartphone in an emergency situation.

212. **Chainsaw:** Having access to a good chainsaw can save you quite a bit of time and labor if you have to scavenge for firewood.

I feel obligated to point out that *while chainsaws can be real time-savers, they can also be very dangerous! If you're going to use one, make sure you get the proper training on how to use them safely and that you wear all the recommended safety gear.*

213. **Chainsaw Supplies:** It would be a waste of your time to keep a chainsaw with your emergency stockpile of supplies if you didn't have the necessary items to keep it running properly. Make sure you have the tool that is necessary for loosening or tightening the chain. This tool is often referred to as a "scrench" because it doubles as both a screwdriver and a wrench.

You'll also want to make sure you have both some round and flat files on hand so you can sharpen the chain when it becomes dull. While you're at it, don't forget that you'll need to store bar oil to keep it lubricated properly. You'll also need a supply of two-stroke oil to be added to any gasoline you plan on using in the chainsaw.

214. **Come-A-Long:** A come-a-long winch is a hand-powered ratcheting device that is used to pull heavy loads. They are equipped with a heavy-duty hook on both ends and high tensile strength wire rope. Much like an electric winch you might find on the front of a heavy duty, four-wheel drive pickup truck, a come-a-long has many useful purposes. They can be used for everything from pulling your vehicle out of a muddy bog to pulling heavy logs you have cut down for firewood.

It's important to realize that when you purchase one of these devices, it will have a recommended load rating. Some are designed to pull very heavy loads, while others are designed to pull lighter loads. It should go without saying that if you use one improperly, you stand the risk of becoming injured if it should break while it's under tension.

Warning: While these items can be extremely useful, they can also be very dangerous if used improperly. If you decide to use one, make sure you follow the manufacturer's recommended safety procedures precisely and that you get the proper training on how to use them safely.

215. **Block and Tackle:** This is an item you may not be familiar with because it's not used much in modern times. In days past, it was a commonly used item because of its tremendous versatility.

In case you're not familiar with this particular item, a block and tackle is basically made up of two or more pulleys and a length of rope. The purpose of this device is to provide you with "mechanical advantage" when it comes to lifting or pulling heavy objects. Due to the way it is designed, a heavy load can be lifted or pulled with much less effort using a block and tackle.

Keep in mind that during a prolonged survival situation you likely won't have access to modern equipment, such as electric winches. For this reason, an item like this could be very beneficial to have around.

One possible example of how you might use this item would be if you have a beef cow that you decide to butcher. With the help of a block and tackle, you could attach a rope to its hind legs and hoist it up so you can hang it during the butchering process.

In a survival situation that you could find yourself in, you may not have the advantage of having several people to help with the heavy lifting. Any items such as a block and tackle that can help you perform these types of chores more easily could be extremely valuable to have on hand.

Warning: Let me offer you a word of warning about purchasing this item. Because this item was more commonly used long ago, you might be tempted to use an antique version that you happen to find at a yard sale. Although you can often find many valuable prepping items at yard sales, something like this may not be one of them.

Since, by their very nature, they are designed to either pull or lift a heavy load, you don't want to risk your safety by using an antique for this type of chore. Instead, you may want to purchase one that is made in modern times to a high standard of quality to prevent the possibility of it breaking and injuring someone.

Always make sure that the rope is of adequate strength to support any loads you'll be lifting or pulling and that it isn't frayed and/or damaged in any way. Also, make sure you always follow the manufacturer's recommended safety instructions when using this type of item.

216. **Tow Strap:** Having access to a heavy duty tow strap can be very useful. Remember, in a doomsday scenario, you won't be able to call your emergency roadside

service and have them send a tow truck out to rescue you.

If your vehicle breaks down or gets stuck in a ditch, you're going to be on your own which is why having a good quality tow strap available to use can be so important. Something to keep in mind about tow straps is that they are rated according to how much weight they are designed to be able to handle without breaking.

Since you're preparing for a doomsday type scenario, it would probably be a good idea to purchase a tow strap that is capable of handling much more than the weight of your personal vehicle, even if you only have a small car. I personally believe that stronger is better when purchasing this type of item.

217. **Tow Chain:** In addition to a tow strap, it might be a good idea to have a heavy duty tow chain on hand as well. One of the limitations of a tow strap is that they are made of a heavy-duty material but they don't handle abrasion well.

If you find yourself in a situation where you need to pull things such as heavy logs out of the forest for firewood, a really strong chain might be a better option because it is less susceptible to fraying and wearing out like a tow strap might be.

Warning: Towing or pulling a heavy load can be extremely dangerous! If the tow strap or tow chain comes loose or breaks, it can become a dangerous projectile that can strike someone and cause serious injury or even death. If you choose to pull anything with a tow strap or chain, make sure you follow all safety precautions, including but not limited to, making sure that the strap or chain is securely attached at both ends so that it won't come loose and cause injury. Make sure that no one stands anywhere near the strap or chain in the event that it should come loose. Also, before using any tow strap or chain, thoroughly inspect them to ensure that they aren't damaged in any way and that they are actually strong enough to handle the load you will be pulling.

218. **Portable Alternative Energy Devices:** Since we may find ourselves having to survive without the traditional power grid, it would be a good idea to have access to some portable solar- or wind-powered charging  equipment. Fortunately, we live in a day and age when there are many options to choose from when it comes to portable alternative energy devices.

You can purchase backpacks with an integrated solar panel. You can also purchase portable solar generators designed to harness the energy of the sun and recharge an integrated battery pack. You can buy portable wind turbines that are designed to be quickly set up and deployed in the field. You can even buy human-powered generators designed to be hand-cranked or pedalled with your feet to recharge your portable electronic devices.

219. **Rechargeable Portable Battery Packs:** In addition to storing alternative energy-producing devices, you may want to consider keeping a rechargeable portable battery pack on hand or in your bug out bag.

A company by the name of Mophie® was kind enough to send me one of their products for free to test and review on

Photo used with permission from Mophie.com

my website, preppersillustrated.com. In my opinion, the product they sent me is ideal for preppers. The name of it is "powerstation XL." After testing it, I can say that I really like it and highly recommend it for preppers. I've recharged my smartphone several times with it and it has performed flawlessly.

It is lightweight at only 11.02 ounces and it measures only 2.80 inches x 4.50 inches x 0.91 inches. Even though it's compact and lightweight, it packs an impressive 12,000mAh battery that can be recharged 500 times.

It's certainly not going to be the type of product that will recharge a dead car battery, but it's not designed for that. It's designed to recharge portable electronic devices, such as cell phones, tablet computers, and other devices, you would typically recharge with a USB cable.

It has two USB charging ports so it can charge two devices at the same time. Both USB ports are reported in the product manual to be capable of outputting up to 2.1 amps simultaneously. It's worth pointing out that the actual device has the following printed on the back of it: "Output: 5V = Max: 2.4A x 2, 44.8 Wh."

After contacting Mophie's customer support, it seems that the device does actually output 2.4 amps despite the manual saying that it outputs "up to 2.1 Amps at each charging port."

If you have one of these devices, you might be able to charge it with a portable solar panel if the panel's output voltage and amperage is appropriate for the powerstation XL. When I contacted Mophie's customer support and inquired about the minimum required power for the device to begin charging, I was informed that it needed at least "1 amp, 5 volts, 5 watts." Again, I would like to point out that the following is printed on the back of the device: "Input: 5V = Max: 1.6 A."

Different electronic devices have their own charging requirements. Mophie seems to have this problem covered. Here's a direct quote from the product manual regarding this matter: "Smart charging circuitry automatically selects the proper charging speed for the connected device, plus built-in short-circuit, over-charge and temperature protection."

You can purchase this product on their website, which is www.mophie.com. At the time this book was written, the price was $129.95.

220. **Paracord Survival Bracelet:** When these nifty little survival accessories first hit the market, they were nothing more than a bracelet that was braided out of 550 paracord, but now you can purchase quite elaborate

versions that have many survival accessories woven right into them.

Some of them come equipped with everything from a compass to a fire starter. The number of accessories they are able to pack into these tiny little bracelets is amazing to me. I highly recommend you purchase one for each member of your family.

Not only do I recommend you purchase them, but it's important you get into the habit of wearing them so you'll actually have them with you should you suddenly find yourself thrust into a survival situation.

221. **Hand-Powered Pump and Hose:** If you find your-self having to scavenge water from a lake or stream, a

hand-powered pump with a hose that can be used to pump from a body of water into your containers can be quite useful. This can help to alleviate some of the backbreaking work that might come from having to carry buckets full of water to your vehicle or wagon from the water source.

As I've already mentioned several times in this book, if you do end up scavenging for water, make sure you properly filter *and* treat it prior to using it.

222. **Calorie Dense Survival Food Bars:** I suggest you consider purchasing a product such as the ER Emergency Ration 3600 Survival Food Bar found at www.QuakeKare.com or 1-800-277-3727.

The reason I like these survival food bars is because they are very dense in calories for their size and weight. They might not be as appetizing as a big juicy steak, but when you are in survival mode and you need to consume calories just to keep going, these items may be extremely valuable to have.

Photo used with permission from QuakeKare.com

Because they are small and lightweight, you can easily carry them while hiking. I don't know about you, but I'd much rather pack something in my backpack that is lightweight and calorie dense than a bunch of heavy cans of chili or stew.

You might also be interested to know that the company which manufactures this product also makes emergency dog and cat food rations. Here's a quote from their website regarding how these pet rations are packaged, ". . . hermetically vacuum sealed and specially packaged to guarantee a 5-year shelf-life ..."

223. **Honey:** Having a supply of honey in your food storage gives you an additional way of sweetening your food and drinks. One of the benefits of storing honey is that it has an extremely long shelf life when stored under the proper conditions.

Honey that is quite old will often crystallize. If this happens, you can easily return it to its regular consistency by taking the lid off its container and partially submerging it in a pot of warm water until the crystals have dissolved.

224. **Emergency Radio:** It's a good idea to have an emergency radio you can listen to so you'll have a chance of being able to receive important broadcasts from government officials and emergency services. I highly recommend that you purchase one that can be charged up by cranking a handle. Some even have a solar panel that will recharge it. Others have a USB port you can use for charging handheld electronic devices, such as smartphones.

225. **Ham Radios:** The ability to communicate with members of your survival party or even other survivors will be very important during a major crisis. Most of us, in this day and age, are quite dependent on our cell phones, but it's best to assume that during a major natural disaster cell phones will not work.

With that in mind, it's a good idea to have some way of communicating and ham radios are an alternative to cell phones. Sure, they're not as convenient as simply dialing a phone, and they do have their limitations, but they are better than having no way of communicating at all.

It's important to distinguish the differences between the basic FRS (Family Radio Service) walkie-talkies you might find at any sporting goods store and ham radios. The manufacturers of these FRS radios advertise ridiculously exaggerated ranges for real-world use. It's not uncommon to see the packages for these types of walkie-talkies claim to have a range of 20 miles or more.

These radios *might* be able to achieve the advertised range under *perfect* conditions, such as when one person is on the top of a mountain and the other person is in a valley and there are absolutely no obstructions between the two that might interfere with the transmission and reception.

Unfortunately, if you ever actually try to use these types of devices for emergency communications, it's highly unlikely that the conditions will be ideal. It's much more likely that there will be obstructions, such as trees, houses, and other buildings, that will significantly limit the range of these types of radios.

The primary reason for this is that due to FCC regulations, these walkie-talkies are only legally allowed to transmit on 500 milliwatts of power. This means that under *real-life* operating conditions, the range of these types of walkie-talkies is probably going to be around a quarter mile to one mile.

Now let's talk about the reason ham radios are a much better alternative to FRS radios. While handheld ham radios are more expensive than FRS radios, you can purchase some relatively inexpensive units that are capable of transmitting on up to eight watts of power. For example, the BaoFeng GT-3TP Mark III tri-power handheld ham radios are advertised to be able to transmit on one, four, or eight watts of power.

At the time that this book was written, you could purchase these radios for around $60 each online. It's worth pointing out that these are entry level handheld ham radios so they aren't considered to be top-of-the-line, but they are affordable enough that many preppers choose them to get their start into the world of ham radio.

Another advantage of using ham radios is that you can utilize what are called "repeaters." A repeater is a device that is usually installed at a higher altitude, such as on a hill or mountain. When you are using a repeater, the signal from your ham radio will be transmitted to the repeater and then the repeater can send your signal back down the other side of the hill. By using this type of technology, you can often communicate over significantly greater distances than you can with traditional line-of-sight communication devices.

You do need a license in order to operate a ham radio. Traditionally, when you had to learn Morse code in order to get a license, but now you can get what is called a "technician class" ham radio license that doesn't require you to learn Morse code. In order to get your technician class ham radio license, you need to pass a 35-question written exam. There are many resources, such as books as well as websites, that can help prepare you to pass the test. Should you choose to become a licensed ham radio operator, you'll only need to renew the license every 10 years.

226. **Camping Stove:** It's probably a good idea to have a camping stove so you'll have an additional way of preparing your meals. If you're bugging out, you might want to select one that is quite portable and uses solid fuel pellets for convenience.

227. **Food Grade Water Containers with Lids:** If you end up in a situation where you have to scavenge for

water, you'll want to have some food grade containers you can use to transport water. You might want to use five-gallon buckets because they are easy to carry, but make sure they are actually rated as being food safe. Additionally, you may want to consider purchasing a product called "The Gamma Seal® Lid." These lids are designed to be affixed to a five-gallon bucket. You can screw on the lid when you want to and they provide an airtight and watertight seal.

228. **Inexpensive Five-Gallon Buckets:** In addition to having some food grade five-gallon buckets, you might want to have a collection of inex-pensive buckets you can pick up at your local hardware stores for a few dollars each. You'll find these buckets to be extremely handy for many survival purposes. They are multi-purpose items, and anytime you can store an item that can  serve more than one function, you're ahead of the game.

One thing that you might not have thought of is that you can actually make emergency toilets out of old five-gallon buckets! I think most people would appreciate having something like this in a survival situation.

229. **Battery Chargers:** You may have the need to recharge automotive batteries so make sure you have

a good 12-volt battery charger. It's also a good idea to have battery chargers that are designed to charge rechargeable batteries that can be used in common household electronic devices.

230. **Rechargeable Batteries:** It should go without mentioning that if you are going to store battery chargers, you should also store rechargeable batteries. Keeping in mind that different electronic devices require different sizes of batteries, it would probably be a good idea to have a large collection of rechargeable batteries ranging in all sizes from AAA to D.

231. **Comfort Items:** If you are doing all you can to survive over a prolonged period of time, you'll probably be quite busy. That being said, there *will be* down time, especially for children. Having a good supply of comfort items to occupy your mind could be very important for your emotional well-being.

For children, things like toys, picture books, coloring books, crayons, puzzles, and candy may do wonders when it comes to comforting them and alleviating some of the fear that they may be experiencing.

For older individuals, reading material, such as magazines, books, and crossword puzzles or other types of puzzle books, could help them deal with the struggles they are facing. Items that have religious significance, such as religious reading materials, can also be very comforting. During stressful times, having items that help individuals feel connected to their particular religious beliefs can do wonders when it comes to helping them cope with the situation.

232. **Tablet Computer:** If you're going to have access to electricity, you may want to consider keeping a tablet computer that has some of your favorite music, movies, and games loaded on it. This is another comfort item that can go a long way toward helping alleviate boredom for both yourself and your young children in a survival situation.

233. **MP3 Players:** Again, if you'll have a way of powering small electronic devices, an MP3 player that is loaded up with your favorite playlist could be quite a luxury in a survival situation.

   If you have a method of recharging these types of devices, such as solar panels or wind turbines, they could be very useful when it comes to helping you maintain your sanity. But, on the other hand, it's never a good idea to use batteries or electricity to power luxury items if energy is in short supply. If you are in a situation where you have a very limited supply of batteries or electricity, it's probably a better idea to conserve your power for more important purposes, such as flashlights, ham radios, or other essential electronic devices.

234. **Rodent Traps:** Protecting your food storage is something you should take very seriously. When it comes to protecting your stockpile of food, you may tend to focus on protecting it from looters and marauders, but there is another threat you need to be aware of: rodents! Mice and rats don't care how important your food storage stockpile is to your family. They will indiscriminately help themselves to anything that is in a container that they can chew through.

Rodent control is something you should be concerned with the very day you store your first bag of beans. Always store your food in rodent-resistant packaging. For example, a bag of beans sitting on a shelf in your food storage room is much more likely to be contaminated by rodents than if you store it in a sturdy food-grade bucket.

Another thing to consider when it comes to protecting your food storage supplies from rodents is to maintain a clean environment. Don't store trash or other items that will attract mice or rats to your food storage area.

Also, you may want to consider keeping traps in the appropriate sizes set and baited. Check on them regularly and safely dispose of any vermin the traps might catch. One last thing, get into the habit of inspecting the area where you keep your food storage on a regular basis for the presence of rodent droppings. If you discover any, this is a telltale sign you have a problem that needs to be dealt with!

Warning: Regardless of what method of rodent control you choose to use, make sure you use them in a manner that won't allow children or pets to be harmed.

235. **Bug Out Trailer**: One thing you always have to keep in mind as a prepper is that there may come a day when it's no longer safe to stay at your home. Whether it's a major natural  disaster that has destroyed your home, or the threat of an invasion from dangerous looters and marauders, you should always have a plan and the means to evacuate quickly.

Many people, including myself, advocate having a bug out bag or 72-hour kit for each member of your family that is packed and ready to grab at a moment's notice. While this is a good strategy for a short-term survival situation, you may find yourself having to survive for a longer period of time.

A bug out trailer can be anything from the 30-foot fifth wheel you can pull behind your truck to a small, lightweight cargo trailer you can pull behind your family sedan. The idea behind having a bug out trailer is that it will enable you to take a much larger quantity of supplies with you if you have to evacuate your home in a hurry.

It may be a good idea to keep the trailer prepacked with nonperishable survival items that you might plan on using. Then, if you find yourself having to cut and run, you can hurry and grab items from your food storage, as well as other items from your emergency preparedness stockpile, to throw in the back of the trailer as you are in the process of bugging out.

When I'm talking about a bug out trailer, I'm not referring to a trailer you use for multiple purposes. A bug out trailer should be like a bug out bag and it should have a single purpose. That purpose is to give you the ability to transport more survival items than you could normally fit in the trunk of your car to your preplanned bug out location.

It should go without saying that if you choose to add this item to your emergency preparedness plans, you must have your vehicle equipped with the appropriate trailer hitch, wiring, receiver, and tow ball in order to safely tow the trailer to your destination.

Sign Up for Free Weekly Updates from Preppers Illustrated

I sincerely hope you found the information in this book helpful in some may. If you did, you might be interested in knowing that I provide a free service where I'll send you weekly prepping tips in the form of an email. I HIGHLY suggest you take a brief moment and sign up now! Don't worry; I won't start spamming your inbox with hundreds of useless emails. I will, however, send you free weekly updates right to your email that will hopefully help you to become a better prepper.

It takes less than thirty seconds to sign up and you don't even have to give me your name if you don't want to. All you need to do is enter your email address on a simple form after going to the URL provided below. If I don't live up to your expectations, you can easily unsubscribe by clicking on the link labeled "unsubscribe" that is found at the bottom of every email I send you.

preppersillustrated.com/sign-up

Please Follow Me on Social Media!

I would really appreciate it if you would follow me on my social media pages. Doing so will mean that you'll be able to receive even more helpful emergency preparedness tips. Besides, being social is fun!

Pinterest: pinterest.com/thepreppermag
Twitter: twitter.com/ThePrepperMag
Facebook: facebook.com/PreppersIllustrated

Don't Be a Stranger!

If you have any questions about this book, emergency preparedness in general, or if you'd just like to chat, please feel free to send me an email at: pattyhahne@ preppersillustrated.com.